THE TOOLS & METHOD OF

TORAH INVESTIGATION

RABBI JONATHAN TAUB

COLOR WAR

Dear Atara,
With a ברכה that you should
soon be a כלה — with no war!
Rabbi Taub

MOSAICA PRESS

Mosaica Press, Inc.

Design by Tsipi Birnboim
Typeset by שחרית

ISBN: 978-1-937887-47-6

Published and distributed by:
Mosaica Press, Inc.
www.mosaicapress.com
info@mosaicapress.com
Printed in Israel

בסייעתא דשמיא

ה שבט תשע"ה

לידידי הרב יונתן טאוב שליט"א

עברתי על חלק נכבד מהספר, וראיתי שהנך מנחיל סימני דרך ברורים ונפלאים להבין ולהעמיק בדברי רבותינו ז"ל בפירוש הכתובים, עפ"י מקורות נאמנים מחכמי הדורות אשר מפיהם אנו חיים.

הדברים נמסרים בטעם ובחן מיוחד, כפי שאתה מוסר בשיעורים בע"פ במסגרות שונות, מתוך רצון להאהיב לימוד המקרא, ולהלהיב הלבבות לעמול ולהעמיק בהבנת התורה הקדושה.

יהי רצון שתזכה לראות ברכה בעמלך, ותרבה הדעת, ומלאה הארץ דעה את ה' כמים לים מכסים.

בברכה,

דברים ברורים ואני מצטרף לדבריו ומברך שיזכה להפיץ מעינותיו שמזכה בזה הרבים.

Letter of Approbation from
Hagaon Hagadol Rebbe Dovid Cohen *shlita*
Rosh Yeshivas Chevron - "Knesses Yisroel"
and Member of the Moetzes Gedolei Hatorah

מכתב מהגאון הגדול רבי דוד כהן שליט"א
ראש ישיבת חברון – "כנסת ישראל",
וחבר מועצת גדולי התורה

בס"ד

מכתב ידידות

הן הראני ידידי הנעלה והגדול הרה"ג יהונתן טאוב שליט"א המשפיע מתורתו ויראתו לבני הנעורים בשיעורים קבועים בישיבות וסמינרים ועכשיו מוציא מתח"י ספר יחודי שתכליתו ליתן את הכלים להעמיק בלימוד חומש עם פירש"י למצוא הדרך להעמיק בדבריו הק' ולמצוא את המטמונים הגנוזים בהם בלשונו הקצר והוא מיוסד על השיעורים שמסר בְמשך השנים בעיה"ק ירושלים ת"ו והוא מלאכה גדולה שיש בה תועלת מרובה גם למורים וגם לתלמידים ולכן מי שמקדיש בזמנו לעיין בדברי רש"י הקדושים בפירושו עה"ת ובודאי יהיה הספר הזה לתועלת מרובה ויהנו ממנו רבים ויחזק לימוד הפרשה עם פרש"י שהוא מיסודי האיש הישראלי בעבודתו והיסוד לכל בן תורה לעלות במסילה העולה בית א-ל

הכו"ח
לכבודן של מנחילי תורה
דוד כהן

הרב ישראל גנס
רח' פנים מאירות 2
קרית מטרסדורף, ירושלים. 94423

בס"ד............סיון תשע"ד..................

הובא לפני ספרו של הרב היקר ר'
יונתן טאוב שליט"א - ספר המבוסס על
שיעורים שמסר במסגרות שונות ועוסק
בלימוד מעמיק בחומש ובמיוחד לימוד
פרש"י ועיקרי אמונה הנלמדים מן הכתובים,
דבר שיש בו כמובן תועלת מרובה.

ולא נצרכה אלא לברכה שיוסיף המחבר שליט"א לתת עוד
תנובה לזכות הרבים בספרים מועילים.

בברכת התורה

זמני קבלת קהל וקבלת טלפונים: 02-5371782 (מענה קולי - עידכון יום יומי). בבית: 02-5378927

בס"ד

From the Desk of

RABBI AHRON LOPIANSKY

Rosh HaYeshiva

2/Nissan/5775

There are four main strata of explaining Torah: *Pshat, remaz, drush* and *sod.* This most unusual *sefer* from Rabbi Taub has done a remarkable job of exploring the *remez* facet of Torah. He does not merely point out tantalizing tidbits as is the norm with *remez* style exposition, but rather weaves an incredible tapestry of meaning and elucidation. Each point that he makes is a gem in its own right; taken together, however, the sum total far exceeds the value of any one observation, scintillating as it may be.

This work is both a fascinating read on its own, and a valuable paradigm for teaching *chumash i*n a way that excites and engages.

It helps the reader realize that Torah is rife with meaning, and within the subtlest of hints the Torah has secreted mounds of depth and meaning. It makes us realize how important it is to study Torah in Hebrew, and to be well acquainted with its grammar. We lose so much of Torah when we do not read it in its native tongue, or are unacquainted with the nuance of l*oshon hakodesh.*

A word of caution. Because of the ambiguous nature of *remez*, one may imitate the technique and then use it to present ideas and points alien and even antithetical to Torah values. *Remez* can only enhance, never replace *pshat.* Only when one is knowledgeable and faithful to the values of torah as presented in *pshat* and *halacha*, may one anchor it and magnify it through *pshat*, as Rabbi Taub has so marvelously done.

May this work ignite sparks of excitement and enthusiasm in those who study it, and may it serve as a paradigm for *chumash* teaching.

Ahron Shraga Lopiansky

YESHIVA OF GREATER WASHINGTON – TIFERES GEDALIAH
1216 ARCOLA AVENUE, SILVER SPRING, MD 20902 ▪ 301-649-7077 ▪ WWW.YESHIVA.EDU

"This book is filled with rare insight and creativity. It is entertaining to read and thought provoking in the extreme. Though it is completely in line with Jewish tradition and rabbinic thought, it nevertheless speaks to our changing and confusing modern world in the idiom of our times. It is well worth having in one's Torah books library."

Rabbi Berel Wein

Rav, Beit Knesset HaNassi, Jerusalem

Director, Destiny Foundation

"It has become apparent that traditional approaches to Torah education are not effective with many of today's students. Creative yet authentic approaches and methods are necessary. Rabbi Taub's excellent book is one example of such an approach and method. It is sure to reach the hearts and minds of many who are otherwise unreachable. Additionally, it offers even the seasoned Torah scholar a fresh perspective on material with which he or she is already familiar. It is the epitome of 'old wine in a new container.'"

Rabbi Dr. Tzvi Hersh Weinreb

Executive Vice President Emeritus of the Orthodox Union

"In his fascinating book, Color War, Rabbi Taub has introduced an innovative and novel approach to teaching and understanding the narratives of the Torah. Despite the originality of this work, it is well grounded in the traditions of the great Torah commentaries and allows the contemporary reader to appreciate the ancient wisdom of our Sages. This book is an important addition to contemporary Torah scholarship and Rabbi Taub's eloquence, clarity and command of the material make Color War an eminently enjoyable and informative read."

Rabbi Mordechai Becher

Gateways lecturer

"A brilliantly crafted book that gets one thinking, then drinking from the deep well springs of Jewish wisdom."

Rabbi Danny Kirsch

Director, Jewish Learning Exchange, London

Contents

FOREWORD

Rabbi Beryl Gershenfeld

Rosh Yeshivah Machon Yaakov

When a modern reader learns Torah, he is often confronted by texts that appear lifeless, opaque and no longer relevant. Thousands of years after Sinai and hundreds of generations removed from revelation the texts can seem cloudy and the message muddled.

A master pedagogue's mission, the greatest mission of life, is to breathe life into seemingly inert texts until they are worthy of our blessing on the Torah: "the life of the world was planted in our midst." What had been a cacophony of notes suddenly becomes a symphony of chords and the listener now hears Torah in its pristine form: "as joyous as when it was given at Sinai" (Yerushalmi *Chagigah* 2:1).

Rabbi Jonathan Taub, one of these rare master craftsmen, brings the Torah to life for his students. He both guides and challenges them by explicitly detailing the textual difficulties, confusing symbols and perplexing conundrums in the text under study. His questions engage the reader and inspire him to use his own mind to grapple deeply with the text. His journey becomes their journey and everyone senses the dramatic challenge of wresting meaning from these wise but riddled texts. His erudition and wit illuminate the path and encourage his students to join the search.

At Machon Yaakov, where Rabbi Taub is a senior lecturer in Talmud, I have experienced his unique ability to elucidate baffling and befuddling Torah texts to hundreds of students while teaching them to turn Torah prose into poetry. His classes are the highlights of students' years in yeshiva and because of his brilliance, passion and dramatic presentation they are remembered for a lifetime.

With this new book, "The Tools & Method of Torah Investigation," Rabbi Taub shares his special tools with the broader public. His questions awaken our desire to search, to study and to know. Why, Rabbi Taub asks, is the wicked Lavan , Yaakov's antagonist, called "white"? Why is the color that symbolizes angelic purity used as a symbol for one who personifies evil? And why didn't you ask this question yourself? The search for meaning has begun.

May Rabbi Taub be blessed to continue sharing the wonders of his wisdom and God's wisdom with those far and near until all join him recognizing that the process of learning Torah even in the 21st century can be "as joyous as when it was given at Sinai"!

Acknowledgments

First and foremost, I must constantly thank the Almighty for having blessed me with the unusual privilege of teaching hundreds of remarkable young men and women, here in Jerusalem.

It is not so long ago that such an opportunity would have seemed a fanciful dream. Even just to be able to live here is something for which many generations yearned, but it is in our times that it has become a reality.

Similarly, many of the students I teach are newcomers to the Torah lifestyle, and this is a phenomenon which only recently came into being.

The chance to learn Torah with these courageous men and women in the holy city of Jerusalem is thus doubly extraordinary.

I would like to thank some of those who have enabled me to teach in their yeshivahs and seminaries.

Rabbi Beryl Gershenfeld and Rabbi Avraham Yitzchak Jacobs established and lead Machon Yaakov, a yeshivah which educates an elite group of dedicated and idealistic young men. The yeshivah is also a base for many groups of university students from America to experience, for the first time, Torah study in a yeshivah setting.

Rabbi and Mrs. Shimon Kurland have dedicated their lives to inspiring and educating thousands of young women in their seminary, Darchei Binah. In fact, the original ideas of this book were developed for a Shabbos retreat which I spent with the students of Darchei Bina.

Rabbi and Mrs. Ilan Segal, who run the Levavi seminary, are special role models. They are not just colleagues, but also close friends.

One of the wonderful benefits of having taught here in Jerusalem is the special people with whom I work. Many of the ideas in the book were the fruits of discussions with one of the most outstanding educators I know, Rabbi Yosef Cohen. Rabbi Immanuel Bernstein gave me many points to consider after he read the manuscript. I also gained much from discussions with Rabbi Uri Sondhelm.

I have the pleasure of learning in the same Beis Medrash as Rabbi Dovid Solomon. He is always available for questions, tracking of sources, and discussion of ideas.

I benefitted greatly from the vast knowledge of Rabbi Pinchas Waldman. He reviewed the entire manuscript and made many suggestions which were incorporated.

I had the privilege to discuss some of the ideas in the book with Harav Chaim Yitzchak Kaplan, one of the foremost Torah thinkers in Jerusalem. He provided the inspiration for section 14.2.

Rabbi David Goldblum, my long-time friend and chevrusah, read the book and made a major contribution.

My brother, Adam, a leading educator in England, gave much input and encouragement.

I owe a major debt of gratitude to my students, for enabling me to try out new ideas and giving feedback. I would like to mention Rabbi Jack Cohen and Evan Weber who both read the book and were very helpful. Mrs. Avigail Kirsh also contributed insights.

Tsipi Birnboim designed a distinctive, striking cover – it was just what I wanted.

Josh Tomaino's advice and help was invaluable.

I would like to thank Rabbi Yaakov Haber, of Mosaica Press, for believing in the book and making it a reality.

His partner, Rabbi Doron Kornbluth, edited the book and totally transformed it. It certainly was bracing to see how it returned after the first edit, but I am truly thankful.

I would like to take this opportunity to express my gratitude to my parents. This book, which focuses on the crucial role of relationships between children and parents, is my way of saying "Thank you."

Finally, to my wife Rachel – I could not do anything without you!

Introduction

Why are people excited by detective novels but not by Chumash?

THE APPEAL OF DETECTIVE NOVELS

One of the most popular literary genres is the detective novel. Often, once the reader starts the book, he cannot put it down until he has reached the gripping climax and has found out "whodunit."

Why are these novels so fascinating? A number of factors come to mind:

1. They have the intellectual challenge of solving a problem, i.e., who committed the crime?
2. It is exhilarating looking for clues that will help solve the problem.

Why are people excited by detective novels but not by Chumash?

3. There is the element of surprise that creates excitement. People are often not who we think they are – there are often hidden identities.
4. There is something very satisfying about seeing the villain receive his just deserts.

WHY IS THE STUDY OF CHUMASH NOT EXCITING?

Many people feel that learning Torah in general and Chumash in particular, is not exciting.

How could this be?

Surely, G-d didn't give us a boring book! The Torah should be fascinating!

Here, too, a number of factors may explain why people do not find learning of Chumash to be exciting:

1. We first learn many of the stories as young children and never progress beyond a childlike understanding.
2. We are never given the tools to understand the Chumash in a deeper way.
3. Frequently, too much emphasis is placed on translation without conveying the beauty of the underlying concepts and ideas.
4. Often the teachers themselves are not excited by what they are teaching. If the teachers themselves are uninspired, few of the students will be.

WHY THIS BOOK?

The ideas in this book are a product of the methods I have learned from my teachers, the interactions with my study partners and the insights of my students over the years.

Together, we will try to share the excitement of unraveling solutions to the challenges raised in Chumash text and the thrill of making amazing discoveries as we do so.

All of the elements which make detective novels so appealing are here:

1. At the beginning, we present several questions and problems which require solving. Subsequent chapters will introduce further challenges.

2. Many of the tools used in plumbing the depths of Torah texts are introduced, including examples of each of the basic approaches – *Pshat* (the straightforward understanding), *Remez* (the approach which discovers allusions in the text, *Drash* (the exegetical approach) and *Sod* (the mystical understanding).[1]

The texts studied in the book are wide-ranging, including sections from Chumash, Nach, Midrash, Talmud, *Shulchan Aruch*, as well as some extracts from kabbalistic sources. Hopefully the resultant panorama demonstrates the interconnected nature of the entire Torah, as well as the opportunity to see a wide array of tools employed.

When many of the tools are introduced, they have been highlighted with background-shading. Where helpful, an example of the tool's usage has been brought.

As a resource for the reader, a list of tools used in this method has been included as an appendix at the end of the book.

Perhaps the major "tool" we have in understanding Chumash in a profound way is the commentary of Rashi. Although various other commentaries are cited, it is Rashi who is most frequently quoted throughout the book, not only his work on Chumash but also his

1. See appendix II. These four approaches are, together, referred to by the acronym פרדס *(Pardes)*.

commentary on Talmud. Both are indispensable to anyone studying Torah. Rashi is the master teacher in how to approach the text.

It should be mentioned that Rashi's commentary on Chumash is almost always prompted by some unexpected aspect of the text, giving rise to the famous question asked by those who study his commentary, "What's bothering Rashi?"

3. There are many surprises throughout the book, including revelations of hidden identities. Hopefully, the reader will be as excited by reading them as I was on discovering them. I have tried to convey this excitement in the book.

However, when teaching a class, a teacher has a number of ways to convey his passion and enthusiasm for what he is teaching. These include body language as well as volume and tone of voice. On the written page these are not available. I hope the reader will therefore excuse what is possibly a slightly more liberal use of exclamation marks than is generally encountered!

4. One of the lessons that clearly emerges from the book is the absolute precision in the way the Almighty runs the world, especially in the use of "measure for measure" in His treatment of man. It is gratifying to see how evil people are punished in a manner which perfectly matches their evil deeds, and how the righteous are rewarded in a similarly fitting manner.

I pray that noticing this strengthens our belief in G-d and His divine providence.

It should be noted that, like with detective investigations, often one needs to follow up leads that appear to steer away from the path being followed. These "diversions" will often provide the most crucial insights. This idea is born out by the teaching of our Sages that "Torah ideas are often sparse in context, but rich in another area." [2]

---

2. Talmud Yerushalmi, *Rosh Hashanah* 17a.

Unlike a detective investigation, though, in which the truth can be ascertained and then the investigation is over, with a "Torah investigation" the case is never closed – the Torah is infinite, and there is always more to be discovered. Continue the detective work on your own – and please share your insights with me!

Let us begin our investigation of some of the most evil men in history.

1
Colorful Villains

1.1 MEET OUR ENEMIES

Two of the most dangerous enemies the Jewish nation ever faced were both "family members" – Lavan and Esav.

Lavan was a grandson of Nachor, Avraham's brother. Lavan's sister was Rivkah, which made him Yitzchak's brother-in-law. Lavan's daughters (Rachel and Leah) married Yaakov.

Despite his close relationships with the Patriarchs and Matriarchs, our Rabbis teach us in the Pesach Haggadah:

> *Go out and learn what Lavan the Aramean planned to do to our father Yaakov. For while Pharaoh's decree applied only to the male children, Lavan sought to uproot all, for it says: "An Aramean sought to destroy my father, and he went down to Egypt and sojourned there as a stranger, few in number; and there he became a nation, great, strong and numerous."*[1]

Similarly, Esav (though Yaakov's brother) planned to kill him. After Yaakov had obtained the blessings from Yitzchak, we are told:

---

1. Devarim 26:5.

Esav hated Yaakov because of the blessing that his father had given him. He said to himself, "The days of mourning will be here soon. I will then be able to kill my brother Yaakov."[2]

Yaakov then flees to the home of Lavan, where he marries and raises his family. When he finally returns home, he sends messengers to Esav, bringing him gifts. Although Yaakov has not seen Esav for thirty-four years,[3] the messengers return saying:

"We came to your brother Esav, and he is also heading towards you and four hundred men are with him."[4]

Rashi comments:

"We came to your brother Esav" – You referred to him as "my brother" but he still behaves toward you as the evil Esav, maintaining his enmity.

There are a number of fascinating questions that demand investigation about these two most evil of men, Lavan and Esav.

1.2 WHAT'S IN A NAME?

One of the essential tools that enable us to arrive at a deeper understanding of the Torah is an awareness of the significance of names mentioned in the Torah. The name of a person or an object in Hebrew, the Holy Language, expresses the very essence of that person or object.[5]

When the Almighty created animals, we read:

Out of the ground the Lord G-d formed every beast of the field

2. Bereishis 27:41.
3. *Megillah* 17a.
4. Bereishis 32:7.
5. See *Yoma* 83b.

and every bird of the sky; and brought them to man to see what he would call them. Whatever the man called every living creature, that was its name.[6]

What is this idea? What is so special about naming animals that the Torah goes out of its way to mention it prominently?

Our Rabbis explain:

When the Almighty planned creating man He consulted with the Angels. He said to them "Let us make man."[7]
They asked Him, "What is the nature of this 'man'?"
He responded, "His [man's] wisdom is greater than yours."
He [the Almighty] brought domesticated animals, wild animals and birds before them [the angels] and asked [about each of them], "What is this one called?" They did not know.
He [the Almighty] then brought them before Man and asked "What is this one called?" Man replied, "This one's name is 'ox' and this one 'donkey' and this one 'horse' and this one 'camel.'"
G-d then asked Man, "And you, what is your name?"
Man replied, "It is fitting that I should be called 'Adam' (אדם) *since I was created from earth* (אדמה)*."*
G-d then asked, "And what is My name?"
Man replied, "It is fitting that You should be called 'Adonai' since You are Master (Adon – אדון) of all."
G-d proclaimed, "I am Adonai; that is name which the first Man called me."[8]

6. Bereishis 2:19.
7. Ibid., 1:26. The Midrash is expounding the use of the plural form. We have written the word "us" without a capital letter. According to the straightforward reading of the phrase, i.e., that the Almighty is speaking to Himself, it should be written as "Us."
8. *Bereishis Rabbah* 17:4.

What does this all mean? In what way is Man's wisdom greater than that of the angels?

The answer is that the name expresses the very essence of the thing being named. Giving a name requires an understanding of the essence of what is being named.

Man could understand the very essence of animals, birds, man himself – and even G-d! – in a way that was beyond the ability of the angels.

Names are crucial. Adam saw the essence of creatures and named them. We can work backwards. It is a principle in the Torah that a name reveals the essence of the person, animal or thing named.

An example from the animal kingdom where we see that the Hebrew name expresses an essence:

Dogs are perhaps the most expressive creatures. A dog will greet its master's return with a wagging tail and obvious excitement. The emotions are clear to see - a dog is all heart.

It is most fitting, then, that the Hebrew for dog is כלב *(kelev)*, a contraction of כל לב *(kol lev)* which means "all heart."

We have learned that names in Torah Hebrew are crucial. They describe the essence of what carries that name.

1.3 WHY THE COLOR WHITE?

The name Lavan (לבן) actually means "white." The color white is generally associated with righteousness and purity.

For example, the prophet Yeshayahu proclaims:

*"Though your sins be like scarlet, they shall be **white** as snow."*[9]

Furthermore, we have learned that when the High priest enters the Holy of Holies on Yom Kippur, he wears "white garments."[10]

9. Yeshayahu 1:18
10. See *Yoma* ch.3, *mishnah* 6.

The question is obvious: How can such an evil man be called "white"?

One might want to answer that Lavan was such a trickster that even his name was a trick – it expressed the exact *opposite* of his true nature.

However, if "Lavan" is the name that the Torah uses, it must reveal who he is, rather than who he is not!

In that case, how do we explain Lavan's name?

As we continue our search for clues, we will make some amazing discoveries that answer the question – and along the way, learn more about Lavan, and the depth of Torah.

1.4 RED SOUP

Yaakov's brother Esav has more than one name. When Avraham passes away, Yaakov prepares a dish of red lentils – customary food for mourners.

> *Yaakov was preparing a dish when Esav came back from the field exhausted. Esav said to Yaakov, "Pour down my throat now*[11] *from this red stuff (*מן האדם האדם הזה *– from this edom), for I am exhausted" – therefore he is called Edom (*אדום*).*[12]

---

11. We have translated the Hebrew word נא as 'now'. The word נא has three possible meanings: (1) please; (2) now; (3) raw, not fully cooked. "Now" and "raw" are clearly thematically connected.
    When a word has multiple meanings, all the possibilities should be considered in translating the word.
    It is fascinating to note that all of the meanings of נא could be correct in this verse. Although Esav is an evil man, he would be prepared to say *please* if that is what is required to obtain the soup. He wants it *now*! He is not even prepared to wait until the lentils are fully prepared, but wants them poured down his throat *uncooked*.
12. Bereishis 25:29-30.

Why is Esav called "Edom" after red soup? The color of the soup would seem to be a trivial element in his life! Names are supposed to reveal the essence of a person's character!

In fact, this is not the first occurrence of the color red in the life of Esav. At his birth, we read:

> *The first twin was born red* (אדמוני)*, completely covered with hair like a hairy coat and they called him Esav.*[13]

If so, why is Esav not called Edom at birth? He is born completely covered with red hair.

Surely that is more significant than the color of some soup that he eats! Why is the minor red reference the cause of his "Edom" name, and the major red reference is not?

1.5 COLOR-WAR

We have seen two strange things about the names Lavan and Edom:

The name Lavan (white) seems to be inappropriate for a scheming trickster.

Esav is called Edom (red) after the color of lentil soup that he eats, rather than the color of his own hair!

One more question – a major one – should occur to us now: Why are both of Yaakov's mortal enemies named after colors? This cannot simply be a coincidence. The question is even more significant in light of the fact that these are the *only* people in the whole of Tenach whose names are colors!

The explanation is remarkable.

---

13. Ibid., 25:25.

1.6 CAMELS AND CAMELS

An important tool used to fathom the depth of Torah passages is the ability to notice motifs and recurring themes.

Consider one example. When Avraham sends Eliezer to find a wife for Yitzchak, there is a recurring motif throughout Eliezer's mission.

> *And the servant [Eliezer] took ten of his master's* ***camels*** *and he journeyed with all of his master's wealth. He traveled to Aram Naharayim, to the city of Nachor.*[14]

When he arrives:

> *He made the* ***camels*** *kneel down outside the city, towards evening, at the time when the women go to draw water.*[15]

He then prays that:

> *"And it shall be that the woman that I ask, 'Tilt now your pitcher that I may drink' and she replies, 'Drink and I will also give your* ***camels*** *to drink,' she is the one You have shown is for your servant Yitzchak."*[16]

Eliezer has not even finished praying when Rivkah appears. When Eliezer asks for a drink, she waits until he has finished before saying:

> *"I will draw water also for your* ***camels****, until they have finished drinking."*[17]

She gives the camels water. When her brother, Lavan, goes to invite Eliezer to stay with them, he finds Eliezer

> *...standing by the* ***camels*** *near the well.*[18]

---

14. Ibid., 24:10.
15. Ibid., v. 11.
16. Ibid., v. 14.
17. Ibid., v. 19.
18. Ibid., v. 30.

Lavan asks Eliezer:

"Why are you standing outside? I have cleaned the house and made room for the ***camels****."*[19]

Eliezer enters the house and then

He unmuzzled the ***camels*** *and gave the* ***camels*** *straw and fodder.*[20]

After Rivkah agrees to marry Yitzchak we read:

Rivkah and her maids arose and they rode on the ***camels****.*[21]

Finally, when they arrive, we are told:

Yitzchak went out to pray in the field toward evening. He raised his eyes, and saw ***camels*** *approaching. When Rivkah looked up and saw Yitzchak, she slid from the* ***camel****.*[22]

There is no doubt that camels *were* part of the story, but the number of times they are mentioned is simply astounding!

While we cannot give a full treatment to this question here, the core idea is that Eliezer is searching for a woman who has the attribute of kindness. This is the reason for the test that he devises – will she offer to give water to the camels as well?

The Hebrew for one who does kindness is גומל חסד *(gomel chesed)*. The Hebrew for camel is גמל *(gamal)*. The camel is constantly carrying for others and yet needs others' help very infrequently, being able to store "provisions" that will keep it supplied for long periods. That is the essence of a גומל חסד – constantly helping others and yet needing little from others.[23]

19. Ibid., v. 31.
20. Ibid., v. 32.
21. Ibid., v. 61.
22. Ibid., vv. 63-64.
23. See, for example, *Kli Yakar* on Bereishis 24:14.

A returning theme or motif is very instructive. Having noticed it, we obtain a totally different depth of understanding.[24]

1.7 FULL OF STONES

We have seen that recurring themes and motifs can teach us much about what is going on "behind the scenes" of sections of Torah.

What is the motif in the story of the encounter between Yaakov and Lavan?

When Yaakov is journeying to Lavan:

> *He came to a certain place and spent the night there because the sun had already set. He took* ***stones*** *of that place and put them under his head and lay down to sleep there.*[25]

When he wakes:

> *He took the* ***stone***[26] *which he had placed under his head and erected it as a standing stone. He poured oil upon it.*[27]

Upon arrival, Yaakov sees a well:

> *The mouth of the well was covered with a large* ***stone****. When all the flocks were gathered there, they would roll the* ***stone*** *from the mouth of the well and water the sheep. Then they would replace the* ***stone*** *on the well's mouth in its place.*[28]

---

24. Another example is the role of dreams in the story of Yosef.
25. Bereishis 28:11.
26. See Rashi, on 28:11, who quotes *Chullin* 91b, where Rav Yitzchak asks that though Yaakov placed "stones" under his head when he went to sleep, on awaking there is only one stone!? He explains: The stones started quarrelling with each other. Each one said, "The righteous man should rest his head upon me." Immediately the Holy One, Blessed is He, made them all one stone. Hence it says, "He takes the *stone* which he had placed under his head."
27. Bereishis 28:18.
28. Ibid., 29:2-3.

Next, when Yaakov sees Rachel coming to the well with her father's flock:

> *He rolls the **stone** from the mouth of the well and waters the sheep of Lavan, his mother's brother.*[29]

Many years later, when Yaakov runs away from Lavan to return to his father's home, Lavan pursues him. When Lavan catches up with him, they make a covenant:

> *Yaakov took a **stone** and raised it as a standing stone. Yaakov told his brothers [sons]: "Collect **stones**." They took **stones** and made a pile. They ate there upon the pile. Lavan called it Yegar Sohadussa,*[30] *whereas Yaakov called it Gal-ed.*[31] *Lavan said "This pile should be a witness today between me and you." Therefore he called its name Gal-ed.*[32]

Stones are a clear motif in Yaakov's life. Why? Why do stones feature so prominently in the story – at the beginning, middle and end? Furthermore, why is the covenant between Yaakov and Lavan made specifically with stones?

Let us investigate. The next step is to try to come to a better understanding of who Lavan is. We will see some remarkable concepts!

---

29. Ibid., v. 10.
30. Aramaic for "pile of witness."
31. Hebrew for "pile of witness."
32. Bereishis 31:45-48.

2 Who is Lavan?

2.1 JUST LISTEN TO ME, DAD!

The first time we encounter Lavan is when Eliezer, searching for a wife for Yitzchak, realizes that Rivkah (Lavan's younger sister) is destined to be Yitzchak's wife. Eliezer recounts the miraculous way by which the Almighty answered his prayer to find the right woman to marry Yitzchak.

On hearing the remarkable account,

> *Lavan [Rivkah's brother] and Besuel [Rivkah's father] responded and said, "This matter is from G-d. We cannot say anything to you, neither bad nor good."*[1]

Rashi comments:

> *"Lavan and Besuel responded" – He [Lavan] was an evil man and jumped in to respond before his father.*

The obvious textual inference which indicates this is that Lavan is mentioned in the verse before Besuel.

---

1. Bereishis 24:50.

A careful reading of the Hebrew text reveals an even deeper level of meaning.

"Lavan and Besuel responded" is the translation of ויען לבן ובתואל. What is unusual about this phrase is that the verb ויען is in the singular, rather than the plural form ויענו.

The use, in verbs and nouns, of singular where plural might be expected, or vice versa, is highly significant.

What is the explanation for the singular form of the verb here instead of the plural?

We find a similar example in the story of Shem and Yefes covering the nakedness of their drunken father:

> *Shem and Yefes took the clothing... and they covered the nakedness of their father.*[2]

The verb used for their taking the clothing is ויקח, a singular form. Why is this used if two sons were involved?

Rashi answers the question:

> *"Shem and Yefes took" – The verb used is not* ויקחו *(plural) but* ויקח *(singular). This teaches that Shem exerted himself more than Yefes in the mitzvah [of showing respect for his father].*

This teaches us an important tool in understanding hidden depths of Torah. The use of the singular form of a verb where the plural would be expected often indicates that one of the people involved was the primary participant.

However, this does not always seem to be true.

When the Jewish people arrive at Mount Sinai to receive the Torah, we read:

---

2. Ibid., 9:23.

ויסעו מרפידים ויבאו מדבר סיני ויחנו במדבר ויחן שם ישראל נגד ההר:

They journeyed from Refidim and they came to the Sinai desert. They encamped in the desert and Yisrael encamped there, facing the mountain.[3]

The first mention of "encamped" is the plural form of the word, ויחנו, whereas the second is in the singular!

Rashi explains:

"And Yisrael encamped there, facing the mountain" – Like one man with one heart.

So now we have another tool:

The singular form can be used to imply a unity of purpose.

When does it indicate that there was a primary participant and when does it imply a unity of purpose?

The Malbim explains that if there are *two subjects*, such as "Shem and Yefes" or "Lavan and Besuel," then the use of the singular implies that the first one mentioned after the verb[4] is the primary participant. If, though, there is one subject, such as "Yisrael," including a number of people, then the use of a singular verb can imply a unity of purpose.[5]

Similarly with Lavan and Besuel, the use of the singular form of the verb indicates that not only did Lavan rush to respond before his father, but that he was the primary party involved, with his father taking a very subsidiary role.[6]

---

3. Shemos 19:2.
4. In Hebrew, unlike English, the verb generally precedes the subject.
5. See Malbim on Vayikra 4:15, para. 250. See also Malbim's *Ayeles Hashachar*, para. 166.
6. See *Be'er Basadeh*, ad loc.

This total disregard for parents is repeated a few verses later. When Eliezer asks to be able to return to his master with Rivkah:

> *Her brother and her mother said, "Let the young girl stay with us for a year or ten months and after that let her go."*[7]

Once again, Lavan speaks before a parent, this time his mother.[8] In addition, note the grammar: "Her brother and her mother said" is the translation of ויאמר אחיה ואמה. Once again, the verb is in the singular rather than the plural form (ויאמרו). Lavan's mother has also been relegated to the sidelines.

2.2 I JUST WANT TO GO HOME!

Lavan's flagrant disrespect for parents is in stark contrast to the approach of Yaakov, who constantly obeys both father and mother.

When Yitzchak intends to give blessings to Esav, Rivkah plans to ensure that Yaakov receives those blessings. We clearly see the close connection Yaakov has with his mother:

> *Rivkah spoke to Yaakov* ***her son*** *saying, "I heard your father speaking to Esav, your brother, saying, 'Bring me venison and make me a tasty dish that I may eat and bless you in front of G-d before I die.' Now,* ***my son****, listen to my voice, to that which I command you."*[9]

Yaakov is reluctant to be part of Rivkah's plan to deceive his father but follows the directive of his mother.

---

7. Bereishis 24:55.
8. An obvious question is why Rivka's mother is speaking now rather than her father, Besuel, who spoke earlier? Rashi, quoting *Bereishis Rabbah* 60:12, answers with the explanation that since Besuel wanted to prevent the marriage of Rivka to Yitzchak, and an angel killed Besuel, enabling Rivka to become Yitzchak's wife.
9. Bereishis 27:6-8.

> *He went and took [two young goats] and brought [them]* ***to his mother****.*[10]

After Yaakov receives the blessings, Esav plans to kill him. Rivkah, who is aware of this, tells Yaakov:

> *"Now,* ***my son****, listen to my voice; flee to Lavan, my brother, to Charan."*[11]

Yitzchak, unaware that Esav plans to kill Yaakov, also tells Yaakov to go to Charan, but for a different reason.

> *"Go up to Padan Aram, to the home of Besuel, your mother's father. Take a wife from there, from the daughters of Lavan, your mother's brother."*[12]

Rivkah's intent is for Yaakov's safety, whereas Yitzchak's intent is for Yaakov to find a wife.

> *Yaakov listened to his* ***father*** *and his* ***mother*** *and he went to Padan Aram.*[13]

He is motivated by concern to fulfill the will of both his father and his mother. He is leaving with the intent to flee from his brother and with the intent to find a wife. He wants to obey the directives of both his parents!

On his journey, Yaakov sees a vision of angels ascending and descending a ladder and G-d promises to protect him. On awakening:

> *Yaakov vowed saying, "If G-d will be with me and protect me on this journey that I am traveling, and will provide me with bread*

---

10. Ibid., v. 14.
11. Ibid., v. 43.
12. Ibid., 28:2.
13. Ibid., v. 7.

> *to eat and clothing to wear, and I return in peace* ***to my father's home****, then the Lord will be my G-d."*[14]

When Yaakov flees from the home of Lavan after spending twenty years there:

> *Yaakov arose and took his sons and wives on camels. He led away all his cattle and took all the goods he had acquired, including everything he had bought in Padan Aram, to return to* ***Yitzchak his father****, in the land of Canaan.*[15]

Think of the contrast with Lavan, who has only disdain for his parents. Throughout his ordeal, Yaakov is motivated by concern to fulfill the will of both his father and his mother. When forced to flee, Yaakov cannot wait to return to his father's home.

The contrast is so great that even Lavan himself understands Yaakov's deep desire is to return to his father's home. He pursues Yaakov, and when he catches up with him says:

> *"I realise that you left because you deeply missed* ***your father's home****."*[16]

2.3 LAVAN SON OF NACHOR?

We have seen that even Lavan understands the close connection that Yaakov has with his father's home. Interestingly, the reverse is also true: Yaakov is aware of the complete lack of connection between Lavan and his father.

When Yaakov arrives in Lavan's home territory, he meets some shepherds.

---

14. Ibid., vv. 20-21.
15. Ibid., 31:17-18.
16. Ibid., 31:30.

> *"From where do you come, brothers?" asked Yaakov. They replied, "We are from Charan."*
> *He asked them, "Do you know Lavan,* ***the son of Nachor****? They replied, "We know [him]."*[17]

There is a major problem in this verse that must be solved! Has Yaakov forgotten his family relationships? Lavan's father is Besuel, not Nachor!

Why does Yaakov refer to him as "Lavan, *the son of Nachor*"?

Of course, Yaakov knows who Lavan is – and that is exactly why he referred to Lavan's grandfather rather than his father – Yaakov knew that Lavan was a man without a father, and referred to him that way!

Lavan *is* prepared to have a grandfather, but not a father.

What is the difference between a father and a grandfather? A father tells his son what to do and disciplines him.

Shlomo Hamelech said:

> *"My son, hear the moral instruction of your father and do not forsake the Torah of your mother."*[18]

Lavan wants nothing to do with a father who will tell him what to do.

Grandfathers, though, do not generally discipline their grandchildren. In fact, they tend to spoil them. Lavan is agreeable to the idea of having a grandfather.

No name, then, is more appropriate than "Lavan, *the son of Nachor*"!

---

17. Ibid., 29:4-5.
18. Mishlei 1:8.

2.4 WE DON'T HAVE FATHERS!

The contrast between the approaches of Yaakov and Lavan toward their fathers is at its sharpest before their final parting, when they make a covenant. Yaakov erects a pillar of stone and his sons build a pile of stones:

> *Lavan then said, "Here is the pile and here is the pillar which I have set up between us. The pile shall be a witness, and the pillar shall be a witness that I will not pass over this pile to you, and you will not pass over this pile and pillar to me, with bad intentions. May the G-d of* ***Avraham****, the god of* ***Nachor*** *judge between us – the god of* ***their father****." Yaakov swore by the Fear of* ***his father*** *Yitzchak.*[19]

Lavan only mentions grandfathers and a great-grandfather. Fathers are conspicuously absent.

Not only does Lavan ignore his own father, but he attempts to influence Yaakov by ignoring Yaakov's father as well. Yaakov's response is unequivocal:

> *Yaakov swore by the Fear of* ***his father*** *Yitzchak.*[20]

He flatly refuses to be influenced by Lavan's disregard for fathers.

2.5 IS THE NAME HOLY OR NOT?

In this encounter between Yaakov and Lavan, there is another plane in which Lavan is threatening Yaakov.

The Hebrew names for "G-d," referring as they do to the Almighty, have holiness. As such, they must be written with special intent and treated with respect. They may not be erased.

---

19. Bereishis 31:51-53.
20. Ibid., v. 53

This is not so for "god" or "gods," referring to false gods. In other words, the same word in the Torah can refer to completely different things – G-d or a false deity. Different meanings will lead to completely different rules governing the word.

We will often have to consider whether a particular name refers to the Almighty or not.

A classic example occurs when Avraham is speaking to the angels who have come to his tent:

> ויאמר אדני אם נא מצאתי חן בעיניך אל נא תעבר מעל עבדך:
>
> *And he [Avraham said], "My master, if I have found favor in your eyes, please do not pass by your servant."*

Rashi explains that the word אדני, "my master," has two explanations. The first is that it referred to the most important of the angels. As such, the name is not holy.

Alternatively, it is read as "my Master" and refers to the Almighty, who had appeared to Avraham. Avraham was asking Him not to leave while he attended to the guests. According to this explanation the name *is* holy.

If we examine Lavan's statement again we find something extraordinary:

> "אלהי אברהם ואלהי נחור ישפטו בינינו אלהי אביהם"
>
> *"May the G-d of* ***Avraham****, the god of* ***Nachor*** *judge between us – the god of* ***their father****."*[21]

There are three occurrences of divine names in the verse. Based on *Maseches Soferim*, Rashi comments:

> ***"G-d*** *of Avraham" – holy; "****god*** *of Nachor" – not holy; "****god*** *of their father" – not holy.*

21. Ibid.

Rashi's explanations of the first two names seem straightforward. Avraham believed in the true G-d and, therefore, "**G-d** of Avraham" is a holy name. Nachor, however, was an idolater and so "**god** of Nachor" is not holy.

However, this explanation of the third name is not quite so clear-cut.

The father of Avraham and Nachor was Terach.[22] We read in the Pesach Haggadah:

At first, our ancestors were idol worshippers, but now the Omnipresent has brought us near to his service, as it is said: And Yehoshua said to all the people: "Thus said Hashem, the G-d of Yisrael: 'On the other side of the river, your fathers dwelt of old, Terach, father of Avraham and father of Nachor, and they[23] served other gods...'"[24]

Furthermore, we know that Terach even manufactured and sold idols.[25]

If so, then the "god of their father," i.e., the god of Terach, is definitely not holy.

However, in the *Midrash Rabbah* we find a conflicting explanation:

*"**God** of their father" – Its meaning is both holy and not holy.[26]*

How can this be true? The *Mattenos Kehunah*[27] explains:

Although, initially, Terach was an idol worshipper, he subsequently repented. We learn this from G-d informing Avraham, "You shall come to your fathers in peace; you shall be

22. Ibid., 11:26.
23. See *Metzudas Dovid* and Malbim who explain that "they" refers to Terach and Nachor.
24. Yehoshua 24:2.
25. *Bereishis Rabbah* 38:13.
26. Ibid.,74:16.
27. A commentary on the *Midrash Rabbah*.

buried in a good old age."[28] *Why is it beneficial for Avraham to "come to his fathers" if they are idolaters? Rashi explains that from here we see that Terach repented.*

So the phrase "god of their father" is ambiguous:

- If it refers to the first part of Terach's life, then it is not holy.
- If it refers to the period after repentance, then it is holy.

We can now understand the statement of the *Midrash Rabbah* that "its meaning is both holy and not holy."

It is not completely clear why *Maseches Soferim* and Rashi disagree. They may reason that Lavan's intent in referring to the god of Terach is likely to be idolatrous, preferring to ignore Terach's change of path late in life. Alternatively, they may argue that any mixture of holy and non-holy profanes the holy and is, by definition, not holy.

Lavan has succeeded in inserting a name into the Torah which is either a mixture of holy and not holy, or is not holy at all.

With what intent is that word in the Torah to be written? Can it be erased?

The truth is that we do not know! We do not know whether it has any sanctity or not![29] So we are in a situation where distinctions between that which we know to be holy and that which we know to be non-holy have been totally blurred.

If one does not have clear boundaries between that which is holy and that which is not, before long there will be no distinction between the two.

---

28. Bereishis 15:15.
29. As such, when a scribe writes this word, he does so with a תנאי, a conditional intent. If the name has sanctity, he intends to write it with sanctity, and if it does not, his intent is that it is written without sanctity.

This is the second manner by which Lavan threatens Yaakov and, thereby, the Jewish nation – the blurring of the delineation between holy and secular.

2.6 A PILE BY ANY OTHER NAME

Another striking example of Lavan's attempt to dilute the distinction between holy and secular is to be found in the naming of the pile of stones erected to mark the covenant between Yaakov and Lavan:

> *Yaakov took a stone and raised it as a pillar. Yaakov told his brothers [sons]: "Collect stones." They took stones and made a pile. They ate there upon the pile. Lavan called it* ***Yegar Sohadussa****, whereas Yaakov called it* ***Gal-ed****. Lavan said "This pile should be a witness today between me and you." Therefore he called its name* ***Gal-ed****.*[30]

As we have seen, what something is called in Hebrew is of the utmost importance. Translations, therefore, are problematic – other languages cannot possibly convey the layers of meaning of the original.[31]

When the pile of stones is erected, Lavan tries to name it "Yegar Sohadussa." This is Aramaic for "pile of witness." This choice of name is not surprising. After all, Lavan is from Aram and speaks Aramaic.

The fascinating point here is that by naming it in Aramaic, Lavan tries to influence Yaakov to do the same!

---

30. Bereishis 31:45-48.
31. There is a fast day in the Jewish calendar, the eighth of Teves, commemorating the forced translation of the Torah into Greek. The translation, although divinely inspired, was a pathetic imitation of the original. *Shulchan Aruch O.H.* 580:2

Yaakov is not to be swayed from single-minded use of the holy language and immediately responds by calling it "Gal-ed" – the Hebrew for "pile of witness."

Seforno, in his commentary, notes:

"Yaakov called it Gal-ed" – Yaakov did not change his language.

There is an allusion in this comment of Seforno to the teaching of our Sages:

In the merit of three practices the Jews were redeemed from Egypt: they did not change their names, ***they did not change their language*** *and they protected themselves from immorality.*[32]

Were it not for these three practices, the Jewish nation would have assimilated and disappeared.

Just as the Jews in Egypt resisted the pressures of the surrounding culture to retain their language, so too Yaakov was resisting pressure from Lavan.

Who wins? Not only does Yaakov steadfastly remain with his language, but he even manages to overpower Lavan:

Lavan called it ***Yegar Sohadussa****, whereas Yaakov called it* ***Gal-ed****. Lavan said "This pile should be a witness today between me and you." Therefore he [Lavan] called its name* ***Gal-ed****.*

In the end, even Lavan calls it Gal-ed!

2.7 UPROOTING ROOTS

We have seen that Lavan is menacing on two fronts:

---

32. *Bamidbar Rabbah* 13:20.

- Firstly, he attempts to sever Yaakov's connection to his father. Listening to one's father means that following the past is important. So Lavan is attempting to disconnect Yaakov from his tradition.
- Secondly, he tries to blur the distinction between holy and secular and to detach Yaakov from his bond with holiness and the holy language.

Note that both of these share the goal of disconnection from one's roots – both familial and spiritual.

Knowing this, it is fascinating to return to what our Sages teach us about Lavan in the Haggadah:

> *Go out and learn what Lavan the Aramean planned to do to our father Yaakov. For while Pharaoh's decree applied only to the male children, Lavan* ***sought to uproot all****, for it says: "...an Aramean sought to destroy my father, and he went down to Egypt and sojourned there as a stranger, few in number; and there he became a nation, great, strong and numerous."*[33]

Lavan does not try to kill directly. He tries to *uproot* – from family and from spirituality. Without roots, a plant cannot survive. Without (familial and spiritual) roots, the nascent Jewish people could not survive.

We have learned much about Lavan. In order to complete the picture, however, we need to look at another of the Jewish nation's most deadly enemies.

---

33. Devarim 26:5.

3

Bilam – swallowing a nation

3.1 WHAT IS BILAM'S REAL NAME?

One of the closest encounters the Jewish nation ever had with possible extermination involved Bilam. He was hired by Balak, king of Moav, to curse the Jews.

Bilam had already proven his ability in the field of cursing by aiding Sichon, king of the Emori, to vanquish Moav in battle.[1] Furthermore, his power of prophecy is compared to that of Moshe:

> *"Never again arose* ***in Israel*** *a prophet such as Moshe"*[2] *– In Israel there never arose, but in the nations of the world there did arise... Who was that prophet? Bilam ben Beor.*[3]

Bilam was effective and powerful. Furthermore, it is clear that he wanted to exterminate the entire Jewish nation:

> *It is written regarding [Bilam] that "he knows the mind of the most High"*[4]*... this teaches us that he knew how to ascertain the*

1. See Rashi, Bamidbar 21:27 and 22:6.
2. Devarim 34:10.
3. *Bamidbar Rabbah* 14:19.
4. Bamidbar 24:16.

exact moment at which the Holy One, Blessed is He, becomes angry. [If Bilam cursed at that moment, the curse would be effective.] This is the meaning of what the prophet [Michah] said to Israel, "My people, remember, please, what Balak king of Moav plotted and what Bilam, son of Beor answered him; [remember the period] from the Shittim to the Gilgal, so that you may remember the benevolences of Hashem."[5] *What is the meaning of "so that you may remember the benevolences of Hashem"?*

Rabbi Elazar explained, "The Holy One, Blessed is He, said to Israel, 'Realize how many benevolences I bestowed upon you in that I did not become angry in the days of the wicked Bilam for had I become angry ***no remnant whatsoever would have remained of the enemies of Israel*** *[a euphemism for the Jews themselves].' That is the meaning of that which Bilam said to Balak, 'How can I curse? G-d has not cursed. And how can I be angry? Hashem has not become angry.'*[6] *This teaches us that during all those days [Hashem] did not become angry."*[7]

Bearing all this in mind, it is fascinating to learn how one of the Aramaic translations of the Torah describes our first meeting with Bilam.

When Balak summons him to curse the Jews:

He [Balak] sent emissaries to Bilam, son of Beor, to Pesorah, which is by the river, to the land of the children of his people, to call him..."[8]

The *Targum Yonasan*[9] translates as follows:

---

5. Michah 6:5.
6. Bamidbar 23:8.
7. *Berachos* 7a.
8. Bamidbar 22:5.

Bilam – swallowing a nation

*He [Balak] sent emissaries to Lavan the Aramean; he is "**Bilam**"*[10] (בלעם) *because he wanted to swallow (*למבלוע *–* ***lemivloah****) the nation (*עמא *–* ***amah****) of the house of Israel.*

We see that the *Targum Yonasan* understood that Bilam's real identity was Lavan. He is referred to as "Bilam," a contraction of the words meaning "to swallow a nation," expressing his intent to exterminate the Jewish nation.

This is problematic. Lavan was alive when Eliezer came to find a wife for Yitzchak. This was in the year 2085 from creation.[11]

Bilam goes to curse the Jewish nation in the last of the forty years in the wilderness. The Jews left Egypt in the year 2448. If so, Bilam was alive in the year 2487[12] – a full 402 years after Lavan had met Eliezer. Although life-spans used to be much longer than today, by the time the Patriarchs were alive we do not find people living in excess of four hundred years.

Is there any alternative to saying that Lavan and Bilam were one and the same man?

---

9. Although referred to as *Targum Yonasan ben Uziel*, this translation was not authored by the *Tanna* Rabbi Yonasan ben Uziel. The Talmud (*Megillah* 3a) only speaks about his authorship of a translation of Nevi'im and Kesuvim, not of Chumash. It is an anthology of midrashic commentary whose authorship is unknown.
10. See *Sanhedrin* 105a where the Talmud also teaches that Bilam was Lavan.
11. Avraham was born in the year 1948 (from the creation of the world). This can be calculated by summing the years at which each of the generations from Adam until Terach, the father of Avraham, gave birth. Yitzchak was born when Avraham was 100 years old, in the year 2048. Eliezer went to the home of Besuel when Yitzchak was thirty-seven years old. We know this from the fact that he went straight after the *akeidah*, which occurred just before the death of Sarah. Sarah gave birth to Yitzchak when she was ninety years old, and died at the age of 127. Therefore, Eliezer met Lavan in the year 2085.
12. 2448+39=2487.

An important idea, which can lead to a deeper understanding of characters in the Torah, is called *gilgul*, reincarnation. A fundamental Torah concept is that if a soul did not achieve what it was meant to achieve, it is given another opportunity to correct what needs to be fixed.

Rabbi Chaim Vital, a student of the Arizal (the foremost teacher of kabbalah), wrote an entire work on the subject of reincarnation, based on the teachings of the Arizal. It is called *Sha'ar Hagilgulim,* literally the gate of *gilgulim*. A *gilgul,* which means "rolling," is the term given to a soul which returns to this world in a different form.

For example, in the prayers we say just before falling asleep, the first paragraph is a proclamation that we forgive anyone who has harmed us, "whether in this *gilgul* or another *gilgul*."

If we know that one person is a *gilgul* of another, we can expect them to have a similar essence!

The *Sha'ar Hagilgulim* reveals a crucial insight:

> *Lavan was reincarnated as Bilam.*[13]

So the *Targum Yonasan* is not necessarily saying that Bilam and Lavan are one and the same man, but they have the same soul and, therefore, the same essence.

How did the *Targum Yonasan* know this? Where are there any clues that indicate this in the text?

Let us investigate the personality of Bilam.

3.2 WHO COMES FROM ARAM?

The first time that Bilam attempts to curse the Jews, his introductory words are as follows:

---

13. Introduction 22.

He took up his discourse as follows and said, "Balak, king of Moav has brought me from ***Aram****."*[14]

There are only two people in the Torah who are described as being Aramean, and we read about them both in the same verse:

Yitzchak was forty years old when he took Rivkah as a wife, the daughter of Besuel the ***Aramean****, from Padan Aram, the sister of Lavan the* ***Aramean****.*[15]

Bilam and Lavan are both Arameans, sharing the same nationality and cultural background. This is the first clue that they share the same essence.

3.3 HIS SON IS BEOR?

The second clue is how Bilam refers to himself and to Balak. When addressing Balak, he says:

"Arise, Bilam and hear; listen to me, son of Tzippor."[16]

The words "son of Tzippor" are the translation of **בנו צפר**. A literal translation of these words would be "his son is Tzippor." Since Balak is the son of Tzippor, we would expect the Hebrew to be **בן צפר**.

Similarly, when referring to himself, Bilam says,

He took up his discourse and said, "The speech of Bilam, son of Beor..."[17]

Instead of finding **בן בער**, the words used are **בנו בער**. Here, the literal translation would be "his son is Beor." This is not true. Beor was Bilam's father, not his son.

---

14. Bamidbar 23:7.
15. Bereishis 25:20.
16. Bamidbar 23:18
17. Ibid., 24:3

Both of these are very strange phrases. Why does Bilam add in the letter *vav*, thus changing the meaning of the phrases and mixing up who was the father and who was the son?

The reason for seemingly unnecessary or grammatically incorrect prefixes and suffixes should always be examined.

Rashi[18] gives two explanations for the seemingly incorrect suffix:

> בנו בער – *Like the phrase* למעינו מים *(Tehillim 114:8).*

Rashi is telling us that sometimes there is a stylistic addition of a *vav* at the end of a word, and it conveys no significant message.

However, there is a problem with this explanation. Adding the *vav* is rare. Why should there be two occurrences specifically in the words of Bilam?

Therefore, Rashi gives a second explanation:[19]

> *Both were greater than their fathers.* בלק בנו צפר – *his father was his son [i.e., inferior] in terms of kingship, and Bilam was greater than his father in prophecy.*

Bilam was proclaiming that he was greater than his father as a prophet and was telling Balak that he was greater than Tzippor as a king. What a public demonstration of contempt for fathers!

In the same vein, note that every time that Balak's father is mentioned, the name is written צפור,[20] i.e., the name is written with a *vav*. There are only two exceptions, when the name is written צפר, without the *vav*. These are the two instances when Bilam is saying the name:

---

18. On Bamidbar 24:3. Why does Rashi not ask this question on the first occurrence of this style of expression, בנו צפר (Bamidbar 23:18)? For explanations see *Maskil LeDavid* and *Be'er Basadeh*.
19. A principle in the study of Rashi's commentary is that when Rashi gives more than one explanation, it indicates that each explanation must have a difficulty which the other one does not.
20. Bamidbar 22:2, 4, 16; Yehoshua 24:9; Shoftim 11:25

ויאמר בלעם אל האלקים בלק בן צפר מלך מואב שלח אלי:

Bilam said to G-d, "Balak, son of Tzippor, sent for me."[21]

וישא משלו ויאמר קום בלק ושמע האזינה עדי בנו צפר:

He took up his discourse and said, "Arise, Bilam and hear; listen to me, son of Tzippor."[22]

When others say Balak's father's name, it is written out in full. When Bilam says it, the *vav* is lacking. Bilam does not even employ the full version of the name!

Similarly, every time that Bilam's father is mentioned, the name is written בעור,[23] i.e., the name is written with a *vav*. There are only two

---

21. Bamidbar 22:10.
22. Ibid., 23:18.
23. Ibid. 22:5, 31:8; Devarim 23:5; Yehoshua 24:9; Michah 6:5.
   It is worth mentioning that certain editions of the Chumash write the name as בער in Bamidbar 22:5, and not בעור. How could this be reconciled with what we have said, i.e., that it is Bilam who uses this form to show his contempt for his father?
   This mention of the name occurs when Bilam is introduced for the first time. R. Tzaddok HaKohen of Lublin (see, for example, what he writes in *Pri Tzaddik*, in the section about Rosh Chodesh Tammuz) and others have explained a fundamental idea for understanding Torah ideas:
   The first occurrence of a name or concept in the Torah is the archetypal example of that word or idea.
   Just as we have seen that the essence of Lavan is that he is לבן בן נחור, so too the Torah may be teaching us that the essence of Bilam is that he is בלעם בן בער, a man with total disdain for his father.
   Alternatively, we have seen that the *Targum Yonasan* explained the name בן בער to mean that Bilam acted foolishly, from the word בער. This explanation is only possible if the name is written without the *vav*. Therefore, the Torah wrote the name this way to convey this idea. A slight difficulty with this answer is that the *Targum Yonasan* writes the name as בן בעור and still explains that it indicates that Bilam acted foolishly! However, this is not so significant since the *Targum Yonasan* never writes the name as בער and, as such, the spelling of the name in the Targum is not a major factor.
   The *Minchas Shai*, quoting the Rema, writes that the correct version is בעור, and that the only two occurrences of בער are when Bilam says בנו בער. He gives a humorous mnemonic to remember which two: יפה כח הבן מכח האב. This is a play upon the words of a Talmudic phrase which occurs in

exceptions when the name is written בער. Again, these are the only two instances when Bilam is saying the name:

> וישא משלו ויאמר נאם בלעם בנו בער ונאם הגבר שתם העין:
>
> *He took up his discourse and said, "The speech of Bilam, son of Beor, and the speech of the man whose eye is open."*[24]

This verse occurs twice, with identical words. In both the name Beor is written lacking a letter. So whenever Bilam says his father's name, he says it with contempt!

Bilam has disdain for his father and tries to ensure that Balak views his father, Tzippor, the same way.

This is a clear indication that we are encountering the essence of Lavan ben Nachor!

3.4 ROCKY MOUNTAINS AND HILLS

Bilam wanted to curse the Jews and, thereby, destroy them. The Almighty transformed the curses into blessings, the third blessing starting with the famous verse, "How good are your tents, Yaakov."[25]

We find that Rabbi Yochanan expounds the entire third blessing showing Bilam's real intentions:

> *Rabbi Yochanan said, "From the blessing of that evil man [Bilam], one can infer what was in his heart [i.e., what he really wanted to curse].*
>
> *He wanted to say:*
>
> *That there should be no houses of prayer or study halls – [and his*

Shevuos 48a, *Chullin* 49b and 63a. It literally means that the legal power of the son, in certain situations, is stronger than that of the father. Here the idea is that when the son is strong, i.e., written in a longer form, בנו, then the father, Beor is weak, i.e., written in a shortened form, בער.

24. Bamidbar 24:3, 15.

25. Ibid., 5.

blessing turned out to be] "How good are your tents, Yaakov."
That the Divine Presence should not reside amongst them – [and his blessing turned out to be] "Your tabernacles, Yisrael."[26]

Rabbi Yochanan continues with each of the phrases of the third blessing and teaches us that by looking at each phrase of Bilam's blessings, we can infer what he really wanted to curse.

Using this principle, it is now remarkable to examine the very first words of Bilam's *first* blessing:

"For from the peaks of rocky mountains I see him, and from the hills I behold him."[27]

What is the meaning of this blessing? Rashi explains:

"For from the peaks of rocky mountains I see him" – I look at their origin, and at the start of their ***roots*** *and I see them with firm foundations, like these rocky mountains and hills, by way of* ***their fathers and mothers****.*

Rashi understands that "rocky mountains" is a metaphor for fathers and "hills" is a metaphor for mothers.

The source of this comment of Rashi is a midrash which beautifully teaches the ideas we have seen:

"For from the peaks of rocky mountains I see him" – This shows the hatred of this wicked man. From the blessings of that evil man [Bilam], one can infer his intent.
What does this resemble? A man who comes to chop down a tree: someone who is not an expert chops the body of the tree, branch by branch, and exhausts himself. The clever man

26. *Sanhedrin* 105a.
27. Bamidbar 23:9.

> *uncovers the roots and cuts [them]. Similarly, that evil man said, "Why should I curse each tribe? I will go to their root."*
> *He came to strike them [the roots] and found them robust. Therefore, he said, "For from the peaks of* ***rocky*** *mountains I see him."*
> *Another idea is: "For from the peaks [of rocky mountains] – these are the fathers; "and from the hills" – these are the mothers.*[28]

So what Bilam really wanted was a disconnection from roots, and no relationship with fathers and mothers. This is exactly the approach that we have seen with Lavan.

We can now appreciate the precision of the wording of our Sages in the Pesach Haggadah:

> *Go out and learn what Lavan the Aramean planned to do to our father Yaakov. For while Pharaoh's decree applied only to the male children, Lavan* ***sought to uproot*** *all.*

We are not told that Lavan wanted to kill or destroy, but that he wanted to *uproot*. Once connection with parents, the life-source of the Jewish nation, has been severed, it is only a matter of time before spiritual death occurs.

3.5 ALL ALONE

Knowing Rabbi Yochanan's principle that Bilam's real intent is the opposite of his blessing, we gain a new understanding into a famous phrase in the Torah – and into Bilam's identity, as well:

> *"For from the peaks of rocky mountains I see him, and from the hills I behold him. It is a people* ***that will dwell alone****, and will not be reckoned among the nations."*[29]

---

28. *Bamidbar Rabbah* 20:19.

Bilam's blessing was that we will be a people who dwells alone. We can infer, therefore, that what he really wanted was that the Jewish nation should *not* dwell alone. His desire was that the holy nation should be intermingled with the other nations of the world. Once again, we see a desire to mix up the holy with the secular!

It is fascinating to see Rashi's comment on this phrase:

> *"It is a people that will dwell alone" – It is this that has been bequeathed to them* ***by their fathers****, that they will dwell alone.*

Rashi understands that this phrase is a continuation of the first words of the verse, which allude to fathers and mothers. The unique holiness of the nation is predicated on the link to parents.

So, in the first verse of blessing we find the same evil intents that we saw with Lavan – an attempt to disconnect from parents and a desire to create a mixture of holy and secular, thereby not allowing the holy to stay holy.

3.6 FACING ENTRANCES

Probably the most famous blessing of Bilam is:

> *"How good are your tents, Yaakov, your tabernacles, Yisrael."*[30]

What was so "good" about the tents? Rashi explains:

> *"How good are your tents" – This is because he saw that their openings did not face each other.*

The entrances to our tents did not face each other. In the end, Bilam was forced to praise us for this arrangement. Working backwards, we can deduce that Bilam wanted the openings of the tents to face each other. Why?

---

29. Bamidbar 23:9.
30. Ibid., 24:5. It is famous because we say it upon entering shul every morning.

When the entrances of tents face each other, there is a lack of modesty and privacy. Men can see the wives of others, privacy is compromised, people who should be external to the intimacy of others suddenly have a "window" into it and borders are blurred. Holiness is mixed with the opposite and thus compromised. Furthermore, there is no more powerful way to sever the connection to fathers than to compromise the sanctity and privacy of Jewish family life.

Although his evil intent was transformed into a blessing, Bilam succeeds soon after in compromising the modesty of the Jewish nation:

> *And [the nation of] Israel dwelt in Shittim, and the people began to commit acts of depravity with the daughters of Moav.*[31]

Here we have the situation where the borders of modesty have been trampled and the holy nation of Israel has been "mixed" with the depraved and sacrilegious Moav.

Rashi informs us:

> *"Began to commit acts of depravity with the daughters of Moav" – It was through the advice of* ***Bilam****.*

This does not surprise us at all, fitting perfectly with Bilam's entire approach.

It is interesting to examine the Hebrew of this verse:

וישב ישראל בשטים ויחל העם לזנות אל בנות מואב:

The word ויחל means "and he/it began." The word can also be read as connected to the word חול, which is the opposite of קודש, holy. Once again, we see the idea of a mixture of holy and profane!

---

31. Ibid., 25:1.

3.7 THE HOLY SPIRIT AT NIGHT

From Bilam's blessings we have uncovered a number of clues which support *Targum Yonasan*'s teaching that Bilam is Lavan. There are several other fascinating pieces of evidence.

When Balak's emissaries arrive and ask Bilam to curse the Jews for him, Bilam tells them:

> *"Stay here overnight and I shall reply to you as Hashem shall speak to me."*[32]

Rashi comments:

> *"Stay here overnight" – The holy spirit only resides on him at night. It is similar with all the prophets of the nations of the world. So too, with regard to* ***Lavan the Aramean****, in a dream at night, as it says, "And G-d came to Lavan in a dream at night,"*[33] *like a man who consorts with his concubine secretly.*

Bilam and Lavan are the prophets of the nations of the world who receive divine communication at night. They have the same essence.

3.8 AN ANGEL IS IN THE WAY

When G-d sees that Bilam travels with the emissaries of Balak, He sends an angel to block Bilam's path:

> *G-d's anger burned because he [Bilam] was going and the angel of Hashem stood in the way to oppose him. Now he was riding on his donkey, accompanied by his two young servants.*
> *When the donkey saw the angel of Hashem standing in the way with a drawn sword in his hand, the donkey went aside from*

32. Ibid., 22:8.
33. Bereishis 31:24.

the way and went into the field. Bilam hit the donkey to turn her back to the way.
Hashem's angel then stood in a narrow path through the vineyards, with a fence on this side and a fence on that side. When the donkey saw Hashem's angel, she pressed herself against the wall, crushing Bilam's leg against the wall. He hit her even more.
Hashem's angel went further, and stood in a narrow place, where there was no room to turn right or left. When the donkey saw Hashem's angel, she lay down under Bilam. Bilam's anger burned and he hit the donkey with a stick.[34]

Why is the angel sent to block Bilam's path three times? Why does the angel stand in three different types of place?

Rashi comments:

"Hashem's angel went further" – What was the reason he stood in three places? He was showing him [Bilam] signs of the Patriarchs.

As we have seen, Lavan and Bilam attempt to disconnect us from our fathers. G-d is sending the angel three times to demonstrate that He was fully aware of Bilam's evil intent.

How do these three places symbolize the three Patriarchs?

The commentators[35] on Rashi refer to the Midrash on which his words are based:

When the angel stood in the first place there was room to pass on either side – "the donkey went aside from the way and went into the field."
In the second place there was only room to pass by on one side.
In the third place "there was no room to turn right or left."

---

34. Bamidbar 22:22-27.
35. See *Mizrachi, Gur Arye, Be'er Heitev* and others.

What is the explanation of the symbolic messages?
If Bilam wanted to curse children of Avraham, he could find what to curse on either side, i.e., the children of Yishmael or the children of Keturah.
If he wanted to curse the children of Yitzchak, he could only find what to curse on one side, i.e., the children of Esav...
Regarding the children of Yaakov, there was no bad progeny [all of Yaakov's children being the righteous founders of the tribes of the Jewish nation] to curse. Therefore, the place is called "a narrow place" (מקום צר)*, an allusion to Yaakov, about whom it says "Yaakov was very afraid and distressed"* (ויירא יעקב מאד ויצר לו).[36] *Therefore, "there was no room to turn right or left."*[37]

In spite of G-d's clear indications of disapproval, Bilam is determined to persist with his plan to sever the connection of the Jewish nation with its fathers – continuing what we saw with Lavan.

3.9 BILAM DOES NOT ALTER HIS BEHAVIOR

When Bilam tries to curse the Jews, he asks Balak to build seven altars. Balak and Bilam sacrifice a bull and a ram on each of these altars.

G-d happened upon Bilam. He [Bilam] said to Him [G-d], "I have prepared the seven altars and I have offered up a bull and a ram on each altar."[38]

What is the significance of *seven* altars?
Furthermore, Bilam mentions "*the* seven altars."

---

36. Bereishis 32:8. The word צר is thematically and etymologically connected to the word ויצר. When one is distressed, one feels constricted.
37. *Bamidbar Rabbah* 20:14.
38. Bamidbar 23:4.

An important grammatical principle is that the use of the definite article implies we have encountered this object, or objects, previously in the Torah.

So "*the* seven altars" implies a reference to previously known altars. What are they?

Rashi explains:

*"**The** seven altars" – It is not written, "I have prepared seven altars," but "I have prepared **the** seven altars." He [Bilam] said before Him [G-d], "The fathers of these people built seven altars before You and I have prepared against all of them."*

Avraham built four:

"And he built there [the plain of Moreh] an altar to Hashem, Who had appeared to him."[39]

"He removed his tent from there to a mountain east of Beit-el... and there he built an altar to Hashem and he called in Hashem's name."[40]

"Avraham removed his tent, and came and settled in the plains of Mamre, in Hebron. There he built an altar to Hashem."[41]

Another altar was built on Mount Moriah [when the binding of Yitzchak occurred.][42]

Yitzchak built one:

"He built an altar there [Be'er Sheva] and called in the name of Hashem."[43]

Yaakov built two:

The first was in Shechem[44] *and the second in Beit-el.*[45]

---

39. Bereishis 12:7.
40. Ibid., v. 8.
41. Ibid., 13:18.
42. Ibid., 22:9.
43. Ibid., 26:25.
44. Ibid., 33:20.
45. Ibid., 35:7.

The intent in Bilam's having seven altars built was to counteract the influence (and altar-building) of Avraham, Yitzchak and Yaakov.

Similarly, the sacrifices offered on them were with this same goal, as Rashi continues:

> *"And I have offered up a bull and a ram on each altar" – Whereas Avraham only offered up one ram.*

Although the forefathers built seven altars, we only are told about one animal sacrificed: the ram that Avraham offered up in place of Yitzchak. Bilam, himself, offers up a ram and a bull on each of the seven altars, the bull being the choicest of sacrifices.

As we have seen with Lavan's fighting the fathers, Bilam is proclaiming that he has outdone them!

3.10 CONTINUITY – WITH NO BREAKS

We have seen that both Lavan and Bilam endeavored to sever the link we have with our fathers and so destroy the continuity of the Jewish people.

However, Hashem thwarted this design.

It is remarkable to see this idea reflected in the spacing of paragraphs recounting the narratives of Lavan and Bilam.

The use of paragraph breaks in the Torah is indicative of a new idea. If a long section is devoid of breaks, the reason should be examined.

In the entire narrative of Yaakov and Lavan, there is not one new paragraph. The entire *parshah* of *Vayetzei*, from Bereishis 28:10 until 32:3 – 148 verses – is one long, uninterrupted piece of text!

Similarly, in the entire narrative of Bilam, there is not one new paragraph! From Bamidbar 22:2 until the end of chapter 24 – 95 verses, there are no breaks. The last verse of this huge paragraph says:

Bilam rose, went and returned to his place; Balak, also, went on his way.[46]

When Bilam departs, then and only then, is there a paragraph break. Having such a structure of no paragraph breaks is extremely rare and clearly comes to teach us an important lesson.

The Almighty's concern to protect the continuity of the Jewish nation is symbolically represented by the uninterrupted Torah text in the stories of Lavan and Bilam.[47] Bilam and Lavan are trying to "break" our connection to Torah and the very text of the Torah itself is teaching us that, ultimately, the connection cannot be severed.

Still, as soon as there is an interruption, the Jewish people are in danger, and indeed stumble. Indeed, immediately after this break, the children of Israel were immoral with the daughters of Moav.

3.11 BLESSINGS OF NON-JEWS

We have seen many parallels between Bilam and Lavan. Consider also that at two important occasions we use blessings of non-Jews. Firstly, when we enter our shuls in the morning we say the blessing of Bilam:

מה טבו אהליך יעקב משכנתיך ישראל:

"How good are your tents, Yaakov, your tabernacles, Yisrael."[48]

---

46. Bamidbar 24:25.
47. It is interesting to observe that there is only one other *parshah* with no breaks – *Mikeitz*. The previous *parshah*, *Vayeishev*, includes the description of Yosef's life with his father before being sold to Egypt. The following *parshah*, *Vayigash*, contains the reunion of Yosef with his father. *Mikeitz* is the *parshah* of total separation from his father, and yet maintaining connection with the beliefs and traditions of Yaakov, as will be discussed in chapter 5. How appropriate that there is not even one break in the entire *parshah* of 146 verses!
48. Bamidbar 24:5.

We have seen that this blessing alludes to "houses of prayer and study halls."[49] The relevance of the verse is clear. Nevertheless, why use the blessing of the evil Bilam, rather than a verse from Tehillim, authored by King David?[50]

Similarly, when a Jewish couple is about to be married, the bridegroom covers the bride's face with a veil. This ceremony is called *badeken*, from the Yiddish meaning "covering." The bystanders bless the bride:

> אחתנו את היי לאלפי רבבה ויירש זרעך את שער שנאיו:
>
> *"Our sister may you be the mother of thousands of ten thousands; may your seed inherit the gate of those which hate them."*[51]

This is the blessing which Lavan and his mother gave Rivkah when she left to marry Yitzchak.[52]

Why, at such special moments, do we use the blessings of the malevolent Lavan, alias Bilam? Consider the question. We will return to it later.

---

49. Section 3.4.
50. A possible "candidate" might have been: "I was happy when they said to me 'Let us go to the house of Hashem.'" (Tehillim 122:1)
51. Bereishis 24:60.
52. The subject of Bereishis 24:60 is the same as verse 55, i.e., Lavan and his mother.

4

Who killed Bilam?

4.1 WHATEVER HAPPENED TO BILAM?

After failing to curse the Jews,

> *Bilam rose, went and returned to his place.*[1]

That is not the end of the story. We have seen that Bilam devised the plot to seduce the children of Israel with the Moabite women.[2] A Midianite princess, Kozbi daughter of Tzur, succeeded in tempting a Jewish prince, Zimri son of Salu. The Jews were even lured into serving the idol, Peor. Punishment quickly followed in the form of a devastating plague.

The only man with the presence of mind to take action was Pinchas:

> *Pinchas, son of Elazar son of Aharon the priest, saw this. He rose up from amongst the congregation and took a spear in his hand. He followed the Israelite man into the inner chamber, and thrust*

1. Bamidbar 24:25.
2. See *Sanhedrin* 106a which describes how the seduction was carried out.

> *both of them through, the Israelite man and the woman through her groin. The plague that had struck the Israelites was arrested. Twenty-four thousand died in the plague.*[3]

Subsequently, the children of Israel were commanded to take revenge against the Midianites[4] and to go to war against them.

> *Moshe sent a thousand men from every tribe as an army, them and Pinchas son of Elazar the priest, to the war, with the holy instruments and the trumpets to sound in his hand.*[5]

The war was successful.

> *They warred against Midian, as Hashem had commanded Moshe, and killed all the males. They also killed the five kings of Midian, upon their corpses:*[6] *Evi, Rekem, Tzur, Chur, and Reva, the five Midianite kings, and they killed Bilam son of Beor by the sword.*[7]

There are a number of puzzling questions here. What was Bilam doing in the vicinity? As we read earlier, Bilam "returned to his place" – and he lived in Aram, nowhere near Midian!

Furthermore, although the verse says that "they killed Bilam son of Beor by the sword," we are not told who actually killed him.

Rashi enlightens us:

> *Bilam had gone there [to Midian*[8]*] to collect remuneration for the twenty-four thousand men of Israel that had been slain [in the plague] through his advice.*

---

3. Bamidbar 25:7-9.
4. As to why they are commanded to take revenge against Midian and not Moav, see Rashi on Bamidbar 25:15, 18 and 31:2.
5. Bamidbar 31:6.
6. This strange phrase will be explained in section 4.2.
7. Bamidbar 31:7-8.
8. As to why he went to receive remuneration from Midian rather than from Moav, see *Mizrachi* and *Gur Arye*.

[Next] he went out from Midian to meet the Israelites and gave them evil advice. He told them, "If when you were six hundred thousand you could not prevail over them [the Midianites], you are now coming to fight with twelve thousand?!" They [the Jews] gave him full remuneration and did not deprive him of his dues [i.e., they killed him for advising them to disobey the divine command to wage war against Midian].[9]

The war against Midian is an act of atonement for the acts of immorality which the Jews had perpetrated, as we read:

Hashem spoke to Moshe saying, "Attack the Midianites and smite them since they attacked you with their wiles, luring you concerning Peor, as well as through their sister Kozbi, daughter of a Midianite prince, who was slain on the day of the plague that resulted from Peor."[10]

Not only did Bilam initiate the stratagem to tempt the Jews, he also tries to prevent them seeking atonement! He wants the sanctity of Israel to be permanently compromised.

4.2 THWARTING AN AERIAL ATTACK

It was not only an army of twelve thousand that was sent to fight Midian:

Moshe sent a thousand men from every tribe as an army [for a total of twelve thousand], them and Pinchas son of Elazar the priest, to the war, with the holy utensils and the trumpets to sound in his hand.[11]

There are several obvious questions here.

---

9. Rashi on Bamidbar 31:8.
10. Bamidbar 25:16-18.
11. Ibid., 31:6.

Why is Pinchas sent?

Why does the verse say "them and Pinchas" – the word "them" would seem to be superfluous.

What are the "holy utensils" and what is their role?

Rashi answers our first two questions:

> *"**Them** and Pinchas" – This tells us that Pinchas was equivalent to all of them [the twelve thousand].*[12] *Why did Pinchas go, rather than his father Elazar?*[13] *The Holy One, Blessed is He, said, "The one who started the meritorious act, by killing Kozbi, should be the one to complete it."*[14]

What about the "holy utensils"? Rashi expounds:

> *These are the aron and the tzitz [the gold band that the High Priest wears on his forehead].*[15]
>
> *These were required because Bilam was together with the Midianites. He used witchcraft to enable the kings of Midian to fly and he was flying with them. He [Pinchas] showed them the tzitz,*[16] *with Hashem's name engraved upon it, and they fell to the*

---

12. This is inferred from the apparently unnecessary repetition of the word "them," which is written to juxtapose Pinchas with "them." It is this juxtaposition which teaches us that "Pinchas was equivalent to all of them."
13. The assumption is that Elazar, the High Priest, was obviously equivalent to all of them. Now that we have learned that also Pinchas was equivalent to all of them, the question is why Pinchas went, rather than his father.
14. Quoting *Bamidbar Rabbah* 22:4.
15. The *Sifrei* explains the inference that the phrase "holy utensils" means these two items is that they are both referred to as "holy." The command to make the *tzitz* uses the phrase "*holy* to Hashem" (Shemos 28:36). These words were engraved on the band. Concerning the *aron*, when the vessels of the *mishkan*, including the *aron*, were being placed in covers for transportation, only Aharon and sons were permitted to be present. This directive is expressed as follows: "No one should come to see when the *holy* is being covered, lest they die." (Bamidbar 4:20)
16. Rashi explained that the "holy vessels" are the *aron* and the *tzitz*. Yet the subsequent description of how Pinchas vanquished Bilam does not discuss

ground. Therefore, it says, "the five kings of Midian, upon their corpses,"[17] *i.e., they hurtled to the ground from the air, landing on corpses [of Midianite soldiers who had already been killed].*

Similarly, it is written about Bilam in the book of Yehoshua, that "the children of Israel killed him, to their [Midianite] corpses."[18] *(The phrase "to their corpses" –* אל חלליהם *would normally be translated as "together with others slain." Here it is explained that Bilam crashed down to corpses already on the ground.)*

Our Sages[19] complete the picture by informing us that it was Pinchas who killed Bilam.

Why, then does the Torah use the plural "and *they* killed Bilam son of Beor by the sword"?[20]

Rashi[21] explains:

He [Pinchas] was the commander-in-chief of the army. Even if someone else actually killed him [Bilam], the whole war is called by Pinchas's name.

Pinchas starts the fight against Bilam by killing Zimri and Kozbi, and continues by being in charge of the war in which Bilam is killed.

By now, it is clear that Pinchas is the nemesis of Bilam. Why?

Furthermore, why is it the *tzitz* that is instrumental in causing Bilam's downfall, both literal and metaphorical?

We need to examine the personality of Pinchas.

---

the *aron*. Why was the *aron* needed? The answer is that the *aron* always accompanies them in battle. This was not the *aron* of the Holy of Holies in the *Mishkan*, but a second *aron* which contained the broken pieces of the first set of tablets of stone (see Rashi on Bamidbar 10:33).

17. Bamidbar 31:8.
18. Yehoshua 13:22.
19. *Sanhedrin* 106b
20. Bamidbar 31:8.
21. *Sanhedrin*, ibid.

4.3 I KNOW WHERE I'M COMING FROM

We learned that Bilam had two agendas:[22]

Firstly, he wanted to sever our roots, cutting our connection with our fathers, in order to destroy the continuity of the Jewish people.

Secondly, he tried to profane the sanctity of the Jews, such that they would no longer be a unique nation.

Pinchas is the antithesis of both of these ideas. He is mentioned by name only four times in the Chumash.

The first describes his birth:

> *Elazar, son of Aharon, took a wife from the daughters of Putiel. She bore him* ***Pinchas.***[23]

The second recounts his taking action on seeing the immorality of Zimri and Kozbi:

> ***Pinchas,*** *son of Elazar son of Aharon the priest, saw this. He rose up from amongst the congregation and took a spear in his hand.*[24]

The third is when Hashem rewards Pinchas, offering him a covenant of peace:

> *Hashem spoke to Moshe, saying, "****Pinchas,*** *son of Elazar son of Aharon the priest, has turned My wrath away from the children of Israel, in that he was zealous for My sake among them, such that I did not destroy the children of Israel in My jealousy. Therefore, tell him that I give him My covenant of peace. It shall be a covenant of eternal priesthood, for him and his seed after him. It is in return for his being zealous for G-d and atoning for the children of Israel."*[25]

---

22. Chapter 3
23. Shemos 6:25.
24. Bamidbar 25:7.
25. Ibid., vv. 10-13.

The fourth and last mention of Pinchas by name is when he goes to fight the Midianites:

> *Moshe sent a thousand men from every tribe as an army, them and* ***Pinchas*** *son of Elazar the priest, to the war, with the holy utensils and the trumpets to sound in his hand.*[26]

If we examine these four instances, we see a very interesting motif. In the entire Torah, there is no occurrence of Pinchas's name without his father being mentioned. This is a man very much connected to his father!

Furthermore, it is rare to find lineage listed in the Torah that includes the names of both father and grandfather. Incredibly, in three of the four instances that Pinchas (and his father) is mentioned, the Torah also mentions Aharon, his grandfather. In the entire Torah, only four grandfathers are brought in the mention of lineage – and in each one there is a special reason.

The first time a grandfather is pointed out concerns Betzalel, who was in charge of building the Mishkan:

> *Betzalel son of Uri son of Chur...*[27]

The Midrash[28] explains that Chur was killed protesting against the construction of the golden calf. His reward was that his grandson was in charge of the construction of the Mishkan, which atoned for the golden calf. Therefore, when discussing Betzalel, in connection with the Mishkan, the lineage is traced back to Chur – it is his merit that caused Betzalel's appointment.

Second, Korach, who rebelled against the leadership of Moshe:

> *Korach son of Yitzhor son of Kehos son of Levi...*[29]

---

26. Ibid., 31:6.
27. Shemos 31:2, 35:30, 38:22.
28. *Shemos Rabbah* 48:2.
29. Bamidbar 16:1.

Why did Korach instigate the rebellion? Rashi[30] enlightens us:

> *He was jealous of the appointment, by Moshe following divine directive, of Elitzofon son of Uziel as prince of the family of Kehos. Korach reasoned, "My father was one of four brothers, as it says, 'the sons of Kehos: Amram, Yitzhor, Hevron and Uziel.'[31] Amram was the firstborn and his two sons took eminence, one is king [Moshe] and the other is High Priest [Aharon]. Who is worthy to receive the next appointment of authority? Is it not me, since I am a son of Yitzhor, who is the second son after Amram? Yet he [Moshe] appointed a son of the youngest of the brothers [Uziel]! I will rebel against him and annul his words."*

The lineage is listed back to Levi to explain why Korach rebelled. He felt that, as a son of Yitzhor, second son of Kehos, he was entitled to be a prince of the tribe of Levi.[32]

The third instance that a grandfather is pointed out is the daughters of Tzelofchod. They are introduced as follows:

> *The daughters of Tzelofchod son of Chefer son of Gilad son of Machir son of Menashe, of the family of Menashe son of Yosef, drew near...*[33]

They were claiming the inheritance in the land of Israel of their father who died leaving no sons. Why does the lineage in the verse go back five generations?

Rashi brings two explanations:

> *"Of the family of Menashe son of Yosef" – Why is this phrase*

30. Quoting *Bamidbar Rabbah* 18:2.
31. Shemos 6:18.
32. Kehos was the most important of the three sons of Levi, so the prince of Kehos was the prince of the tribe of Levi.
33. Bamidbar 27:1.

> *written, it has already said "son of Menashe"? It is to teach us that just as Yosef loved the land [of Israel], requesting "you shall take my bones up with you from here" [i.e., from Egypt to Israel],*[34] *so too his descendants loved the land, requesting "give us a portion of land."*
>
> *Also it teaches us that they were all righteous: anyone about whom we do not know whether they or their ancestors were righteous, and one person in the chain of lineage is known to be righteous, this tells us that the entire chain is righteous.*

The end of the story of the daughters of Tzelofchod contains a final example:

> *The chief fathers of the family of Gilad, son of Machir, son of Menashe of the families of the sons of Yosef, drew near...*[35]

The family chiefs are coming to express their concern that the daughters of Tzelofchod will marry out of the tribe, and since inheritance is patrilineal, their lands will transfer to other tribes. Mentioning the family lineage is thus very appropriate.[36]

We have seen that any mention of grandfathers in lineage is both rare and highly significant.

Why do find this with Pinchas, and more than once?

We saw that Rashi wrote, in connection with the daughters of Tzelofchod:

> *Anyone about whom we do not know whether they or their ancestors were righteous, and one person in the chain of*

---

34. Bereishis 50:25.
35. Bamidbar 36:1.
36. Interestingly, Rashi does not comment on this verse at all. It could be that both of Rashi's explanations concerning the daughters of Tzelofchod apply here as well. The concern of the family chiefs stemmed from a sincere love of the land of Israel and the Torah is teaching us that they were genuinely righteous.

lineage is known to be righteous, this tells us that the entire chain is righteous.

According to this, one explanation for the mention of Aharon is to teach us that Pinchas was "a righteous man, the son of a righteous man, the son of a righteous man" and was only motivated by concern for the glory of Heaven.[37]

Rashi teaches us another idea:

"Pinchas, son of Elazar son of Aharon the priest" - The tribes were demonstrating their contempt for him, saying, "Have you seen this son of Puti, whose mother's father fattened calves for

---

37. *Midrash Lekach Tov, parshas Balak.*
Since we have already encountered the concept of *gilgul*, reincarnation (see section 3.1), and in the light of the fact that that we will be learning about it extensively in chapters 16, 17 and 18, it is fascinating to see the explanation of the *Zohar* for the mention of Aharon in the lineage of Pinchas.
The *Zohar* (*Pinchas* p. 217a) recounts that when Pinchas killed Zimri, one of the princes of the tribe of Shimon, many of that tribe tried to kill Pinchas. When he saw them approaching, his soul left him out of fear. Thinking he was dead, they went away. Then the two souls of Nadav and Avihu entered the body of Pinchas together with the soul of Pinchas.
Nadav and Avihu were the two sons of Aharon who had died bringing incense into the Mishkan without being commanded to do so. They were mistaken in this action. Their reincarnation is in the body of Pinchas, who had killed Zimri without being commanded to do so. In fact, if he had asked Moshe whether he should do so, the answer would have been "No." Yet he acted correctly, as the Almighty testifies. So the body of Pinchas is the appropriate place to find a *tikkun*, a correction, for acting *incorrectly* without a command.
Interestingly, the *Zohar* (*Acharei* p. 57b) asks the question why *two* souls entered *one* body rather than two, and answers that since Nadav and Avihu had not married, they are only considered half souls, and as such, they are only one soul in total.
We can now understand why Pinchas is referred to as "Pinchas, son of Elazar son of Aharon the priest." He is Pinchas, who is "son of Elazar," and also contains the souls of Nadav and Avihu, who are sons of "Aharon the priest." So Pinchas is both a son of his father Elazar and a son of his grandfather Aharon! (*Zohar*, *Pinchas* p. 217a.)

idol worship, and he went and killed a prince of one of the tribes of Israel!" Therefore, the verse shows his lineage to Aharon.

This comment of Rashi is alluding to the verse where we learned about the birth of Pinchas:

Elazar, son of Aharon, took a wife from the daughters of Putiel. She bore him Pinchas.[38]

Who was Putiel? Rashi gives us two opinions:

"From the daughters of Putiel (פוטיאל)*" – From the descendants of Yisro who fattened* (שפטם) *calves for idol worship, and from the descendants of Yosef who showed contempt* (שפטפט) *for his evil inclination.*

Since there was derision of Pinchas and doubt as to the correctness of his course of action due to the idolatry of his ancestor, Yisro, there was a need to remind us that he was also a grandson of Aharon, about whom Hillel said:

"Be disciples of Aharon, love peace and pursue peace, love people and draw them close to Torah."[39]

The Torah wanted to point out to us that Pinchas was not motivated by any alien considerations, only by a genuine desire for peace.

In the light of what we have learned about Bilam, perhaps there is another dimension to the significance of constantly referring to the father and grandfather of Pinchas.

Bilam was trying to sever connection to fathers and to destroy continuity. It is totally appropriate that his nemesis is a man who is

---

38. Shemos 6:25.
39. *Avos* 1:12.

never mentioned without the name of his father and, three out of four times that the name "Pinchas" is written, his grandfather is mentioned as well. He is the most connected of men!

With this insight, it is fascinating to see the second explanation of Rashi as to why Pinchas goes out to battle against Midian. We saw that the first explanation was:

> *The Holy One, Blessed is He, said, "The one who started the meritorious act, by killing Kozbi, should be the one to complete it."*[40]

Rashi then writes a second explanation:

> *He went to avenge the vengeance of Yosef, his maternal grandfather,*[41] *as it says, "The Medonim sold him [Yosef]."*[42]

The word "Medonim" means the same as "Midyonim," i.e., people from Midian. It was people from Midian who sold Pinchas's grandfather.

His connection to fathers inspires him to redress the wrong perpetrated against Yosef!

4.4 THE BAND THAT BROUGHT THEM DOWN

We know that, besides trying to terminate continuity, Bilam tries to pollute the sanctity of the Jewish nation by the seduction of the Jewish men.

How does Pinchas fight this?

Firstly, as we saw, he kills a Jewish leader involved in this pollution.

---

40. Rashi on Bamidbar 31:6, quoting *Bamidbar Rabbah* 22:4.
41. See Rashi, ad loc., for a proof that Yosef was the maternal grandfather of Pinchas.
42. Bereishis 37:36.

Then, in the battle against Midian and Bilam, Pinchas takes the *tzitz*, the gold band worn on the forehead of the High Priest. Why was the *tzitz* the weapon which Pinchas used?

The command to make the *tzitz* says:

> *Make a forehead-band (tzitz)... and engrave on it in the same manner as a signet ring, "**Holy** to Hashem"...it shall be worn on Aharon's forehead... it shall be on his forehead **continuously**...*[43]

Could it really be worn "continuously"? It was only worn during priestly service!

Rashi[44] explains:

> *This teaches us that while it was on his forehead, he would touch it from time to time so that he would not lose awareness of it.*

The *tzitz* was, both literally and metaphorically, constantly on his mind.

Now we understand why the *tzitz* is the weapon that overcomes Bilam. The *tzitz* epitomizes the ideas of unbroken connection to holiness, the absolute symbol of all that Bilam is trying to destroy.

4.5 ETERNAL REWARD

A key concept in understanding how the Almighty runs the world is that of "measure for measure." This applies to both divine retribution and reward. The retribution must match the sin and the reward must match the action that it rewards. This concept is often encountered in Torah and is a major tool in comprehending why particular punishments are meted out and why specific rewards are given.

43. Shemos 28:36-38.
44. Quoting *Yoma* 7b.

If we examine the rewards Pinchas receives, we see a remarkable demonstration of this idea.

> *Hashem spoke to Moshe, saying, "Pinchas, son of Elazar son of Aharon the priest, has turned my wrath away from the children of Israel, in that he was zealous for my sake among them, such that I did not destroy the children of Israel in my jealousy. Therefore, tell him that I give him My covenant of peace. It shall be a covenant of eternal priesthood, for him and his seed after him. It is in return for his being zealous for G-d and atoning for the children of Israel."*[45]

What is the "covenant of eternal priesthood"?

Rashi explains:

> *"Covenant of eternal priesthood" – Even though the priesthood had already been given to the descendants of Aharon [and Pinchas was a grandson of Aharon], it had only been conferred on Aharon and his sons who had been anointed with him, and on any descendants who would be born subsequently. Pinchas was already alive and had not been anointed.*
>
> *As such, he would not have been a priest. As we have learned in tractate Zevachim,*[46] *"Pinchas did not become a priest until he killed Zimri."*

For opposing the man who tries to defile the sanctity of the Jewish people, Pinchas becomes a priest, one who performs the *holy* service.

Bilam also tried to prevent continuity from fathers to sons. Therefore, Pinchas receives "a covenant of *eternal* priesthood, for him and *his seed after him*." The covenant will pass from father to son, forever.

---

45. Bamidbar 25:10-13.
46. *Zevachim* 101b.

With understanding about Pinchas and his leadership in the battle against Bilam, we can appreciate how appropriate it is that there is a view that Eliyahu Hanavi is Pinchas. Rashi[47] explains:

> *Concerning Eliyahu it says, "I was zealous [for Hashem, G-d of Hosts]"*[48] *and concerning Pinchas it says, "He was zealous for My sake."*[49]

The use of these similar phrases is understood to mean that they are one and the same man. As our Rabbis teach us:

> *Eliyahu is still alive.*[50]

Eliyahu will usher in the advent of Moshiach,[51] and thus Pinchas, the man who fights for continuity, lives forever.

Not only that, but when Jews enter a "holy covenant"[52] with the Almighty, when *milah* is performed, it is Pinchas, alias Eliyahu, who is always present.

The Midrash[53] teaches us:

> *The Holy One, Blessed is He, said to Eliyahu, "You are always zealous for Me. You were zealous at Shittim when immorality took place, as it says, 'Pinchas, son of Elazar son of Aharon the priest... was zealous for my sake,'*[54] *and here*[55] *you were*

---

47. *Bava Metzia* 114b, s.v. *lav Kohen mar.*
48. I Melachim 19:10, 14. This refers to the contest with the prophets of Baal.
49. Bamidbar 25:11.
50. *Bava Basra* 121b.
51. *Eiruvin* 43b.
52. This phrase is part of the blessing we recite immediately after *milah* has been performed. See *Shabbos* 137b.
53. *Pirkei D'Rebbe Eliezer*, ch. 28; *Yalkut Shimoni, Bereishis remez* 71.
54. Bamidbar 25:11.
55. The connection with *milah* is that Eliyahu said, after vanquishing the false prophets, "קנא קנאתי לה' אלהי צבאות כי עזבו בריתך בני ישראל" – "I was very zealous for Hashem, G-d of Hosts, for the children of Yisrael have forsaken Your *covenant*." (I Melachim 19:10) The word "covenant" is understood by

zealous. By your life, no bris milah will happen until you are there to see it yourself."
This is the reason that Chazal instituted having a distinguished chair (at a bris milah) for the angel of covenant, known as "Eliyahu, of blessed memory, the angel of covenant," as it says "the angel of covenant whom you desire."[56]

Pinchas, who stood up for continuity, receives an eternal covenant, for himself and his descendants. This is perfectly fitting as a reward for opposing Bilam's attempt to destroy continuity.

For opposing the desecration of the sanctity of the Jewish nation, Pinchas is appointed one who performs the *holy* service of G-d and, as Eliyahu, is always present when a "*holy* covenant" is initiated. Totally appropriate!

---

the Midrash as referring to the covenant of *milah*, which had been under threat.

56. Malachi 3:1.

5

Yosef and a glimpse in the window

5.1 TWENTY-TWO YEARS APART

We have seen that Lavan tries to sever Yaakov's bond with his father. It would seem that he did not succeed.[1]

When Yaakov sends messengers to Esav, he instructs them to tell his brother:

> *Your servant, Yaakov, says: I have dwelt* (גרתי) *with Lavan and I delayed my return until now.*[2]

Rashi, in his second interpretation of the word גרתי writes:

> גרתי *has the numerical value 613* (תרי"ג), [3] *i.e., [Yaakov] is saying, "Although I dwelt with the evil Lavan, I kept the 613 commandments, not learning from his evil ways."*

---

1. See section 2.4.
2. Bereishis 32:5.

In truth, though, the observance of *one* commandment *had* been compromised.

Years later, when Yaakov thinks that Yosef has been killed by a wild animal:

> *Yaakov tore his robes in grief and put on sackcloth. He mourned for his son for many days.*[4]

What are "many days"? Rashi explains:

> *"Many days" – Twenty-two years, from when [Yosef] was separated from him until Yaakov went down to Egypt [to be reunited with Yosef]. We know this to be so, since "Yosef was seventeen years old"*[5] *[when the brothers sold him]; "Yosef was thirty years old when he stood before Pharaoh";*[6] *there were seven years of plenty* [7]*and two years of famine, before Yaakov arrived in Egypt. This gives us a total of twenty-two years.*
> *These correspond to the twenty-two years that* ***Yaakov did not fulfill the commandment to honor parents:***[8] *he spent twenty years in Lavan's home and two years on the journey back from Lavan's home, one and a half years in Sukkos and six months in Bet-el.*[9]

---

3. This is the number of commandments in the Torah. See *Makkos* 23b. For an explanation of the tool of using the numerical value of letters, *gematria*, see section 10.14.
4. Bereishis 37:34.
5. Ibid., 37:2.
6. Ibid., 41:46.
7. Ibid., v. 47.
8. How was Yaakov remiss in honoring parents – they had told him to go to Padan Aram (see section 2.2)! *Sifsei Chachamim*, quoting Rabbeinu Bechhaye, explains that their intent was that he should marry Leah and return immediately. Yaakov, though, loved Rachel because of her beauty, and offered Lavan, "I will work seven years for Rachel" (Bereishis 29:18). Therefore, all the time Yaakov spent there is considered of his own volition. See also *Be'er Basadeh*.
9. *Megillah* 17a.

This is what Yaakov meant when he told Lavan, "This is ***to me*** *twenty years in your house"*[10] *– they are* ***my*** *years, I am culpable for them and am destined to be punished for them.*

In the end, Lavan *did* cause a rupture between Yaakov and his parents. The punishment for Yaakov, measure for measure, is that he loses his beloved Yosef for twenty-two years!

5.2 NON-STOP SEDUCTION

During those twenty-two years, Yosef is almost irreparably lost to his father. He is sold to Potiphar, and before long:

His master's wife cast her eyes upon Yosef. She said, "Lie with me." He absolutely refused. He said to his master's wife, "Behold, my master does not even know what I do in the house. He has entrusted me with everything he owns. There is no one greater in this house than me. He has kept nothing back from me, except for you, his wife. How could I do such a great wrong? I would be sinning against G-d."[11]

The Midrash expounds upon Yosef's reasoning for his refusal:

He said, "Behold my Master"[12] *– "The Holy One, Blessed is He, is known to choose one of the beloved members of my father's house*[13] *as a sacrifice. [G-d told Avraham, "Take your son... and*

10. Bereishis 31:41.
11. Ibid., 39:7-9
12. The textual inference is the words "Behold my master," which is now understood as not referring to Potiphar, but the Almighty.
13. The inference is from the words "There is no one greater in this house than me," the house now being interpreted to refer to his father's house.

> *offer him up."]*[14] *If I listen to you, perhaps I might be selected, and I will be invalid*[15] *as a sacrifice."*[16]

Yosef understands that what is at stake is both a connection to his father's home and a level of sanctity such that he could be a sacrifice to the Almighty. Notice that these are the two very areas (continuity and sanctity) that Lavan attacks! Yosef is part of this epic struggle. He is in this situation because Lavan managed to keep Yaakov away from his parents for those twenty-two years.

Potiphar's wife was not to be deterred:

> *She spoke to Yosef every day, but he would not listen to her, to lie with her or to be with her. One such day, he came into the house to do his work. None of the men of the household were there in the house. She grabbed him by his garment, saying, "Lie with me!" He fled, leaving his garment in her hand, and went outside.*[17]

Chazal teach us that she tried every means possible, from friendly persuasion to threats of torture.[18] She almost succeeded. We learn in the Talmud:

> *"He came into the house to do his work"*[19] *– Rav and Shmuel disagreed as to what this means. One explained that it means literally "his work" [i.e., the work he had to do in the house]; the other explained it euphemistically, to do what he needed to do [with her].*[20]

---

14. Bereishis 22:2
15. The inference is from the words "He has kept nothing back from me." The Hebrew is **ולא חשך ממני מאומה**, the word מאומה resembling the word מום, meaning "a blemish." See Rashi, Bereishis 22:12.
16. *Bereishis Rabbah* 87:5.
17. Bereishis 39:10-12.
18. See *Yalkut Shimoni, Bereishis remez* 145; *Bereishis Rabbah* 87:10.
19. Bereishis 39:11.
20. *Sota* 36b, Rashi, ad loc.

How did Yosef manage to resist such an onslaught? We need to examine the blessing Yosef receives from his father, just before Yaakov dies.

5.3 AN IMAGE IN THE WINDOW

In his final blessing to Yosef, Yaakov alludes to the episode in which Yosef resisted the temptation of Potiphar's wife:

> *"His bow remained firm, his arms were bedecked with gold, from the Mighty One of Yaakov, from there he became a shepherd, a stone of Yisrael."*[21]

This verse is complex and replete with allusions. Rashi[22] explains:

The phrase "his bow remained firm" is a euphemistic expression for the fact that Yosef resisted temptation.

The words "his arms were bedecked with gold" refer to the gold ring Pharaoh placed on his hand, signifying his appointment to be in charge of governance. There is also a euphemistic allusion to Yosef's determination not to be subdued by Potiphar's wife.

The words "the Mighty One (אביר) of Yaakov" have two possible meanings. If the previous phrase, "his arms were bedecked with gold" refers to the gold ring Pharaoh placed on Yosef's hand, then this phrase is a reference to the Holy One, Blessed is He, who brought this about.

If, though, the previous phrase refers to Yosef's triumph over temptation, then this phrase, אביר יעקב, refers to Yaakov himself, i.e., it does not mean "[G-d] – the Mighty One of Yaakov," but rather "the mighty one, Yaakov."

In other words, Yosef's triumph over temptation was due to the help of his father. How was this so?

---

21. Bereishis 49:24
22. On verses 24 and 26.

Chazal taught:

> *"She grabbed him by his garment"*[23] *– At that moment the image of his father came, appeared to him in the window,*[24] *and said, "Your brothers are destined to have their names engraved on the stones of the ephod, and your name is meant to be with them. Do you want your name to be effaced from being among them? You will be known as 'one who keeps company with harlots', as it is written, 'one who keeps company with harlots will lose much wealth.'"*[25] *Immediately, "his bow remained firm"*[26] *(i.e., Yosef resisted temptation).*[27]

We have seen:

- Lavan tries to sever Yaakov's link with his father.
- By "keeping" Yaakov with him, he succeeds in preventing Yaakov from properly honoring his father for twenty-two years.
- Measure for measure, Yaakov is punished with separation from Yosef for twenty-two years.
- During that time, Yosef is almost eternally lost to his father.
- Most appropriately, it is Yosef's relationship with his father that saves him when he is most under threat. Lavan attacked the continuity and *kedushah* of Yaakov and it was that very continuity that saved Yosef's connection and *kedushah*.

---

23. Bereishis 39:12.
24. What inference is there in the Torah text to indicate this? Tosfos (*Sota* 36b) give the explanation of R. Moshe Hadarshan, that the phrase "none of the men of the household were there in the house" implies that there *was* a man present who was *not* of the household (because if this were not so it was have sufficed to write "no man was in the house") and this man was Yaakov. How do we know that the image was "in the window"? The inference may be from the phrase "in the house," implying there was no one else in the house, but there was outside the house.
25. Mishlei 29:3.
26. Bereishis 49:24.
27. *Sotah* 36b.

6

Stone of Yisrael

6.1 STONE OF YISRAEL

We saw that it was the prospect of not having his name on a stone of the *ephod* which helped Yosef resist Potiphar's wife. What does this mean?

Also, what did Yaakov mean when he blessed Yosef, "From there he became a shepherd, a stone of Yisrael"?[1]

The idea of being "a shepherd" is straightforward. Yosef is the one who will provide the family with sustenance during the years of famine.

What, though, does "stone of Yisrael" mean?

A crucial clue in resolving many of the questions we have asked is a short comment of Rashi:

> *"Stone (אבן) of Yisrael" – This is a contraction of "father" (אב) and "son" (בן); [the Targum translates the word אבן as] "fathers and sons," – Yaakov and sons.*[2]

1. Bereishis 49:24.
2. Ad loc.

This introduces us to a tool which we will often encounter: a word, or name, may be a contraction of a number of smaller words.

In return for connection to his father, Yosef will be a "stone of Yisrael." What is the significance of a stone? What is its association with "fathers and sons"?

6.2 THE ALEPH-BEIS ABOUT FATHERS

What is the role of a father?

R. Samson Raphael Hirsch explains:

> *Our tradition depends on the faithful transmission by parents to children, and on the willing acceptance by children from the hands of their parents... without this bond, the chain of generations is broken, the Jewish past is lost for the future – and the Jewish nation ceases to exist.*[3]

Without a father, there is no connection to our tradition. That is one of the reasons that a father is called אב – if there is no father, then there is not even *aleph-beis*, א–ב. In other words, without tradition being passed down from generation to generation, there is nothing.

6.3 SONS WHO BUILD

A father is called אב (the first two letters of the *aleph-beis*) to show that everything begins with a father.

Why is a son called בן?

The final letter of אב is ב. The first letter of בן is ב, i.e., the son continues where the father concluded.

The second letter of בן is ן *(nun)*.

The final *nun* is the longest, straightest letter in the *aleph-beis* and

3. Commentary on Shemos 20:12.

thus connotes continuity. For example, one who learns is called a לומד. When the ן is added we obtain the word למדן, who is constantly and deeply involved with study. Similarly, one who is angry is called כועס. Adding the ן gives us כעסן, who is habitually angry.

In other words, the word בן conveys the idea that the son takes the path of the father – and stays on it.

We can now understand why the word for "son," בן, has the same root as the word for "builds," בונה. The son builds on the achievements of his father, continuing the same way without deviation.

6.4 BUILDING BLOCKS OF THE JEWISH NATION

As we have seen, Hebrew names reveal remarkable depths:

אב *(av)*, father, means the beginning, the source.

בן *(ben)*, son, means the faithful continuation of the father's path.

When you combine them (a father transmitting a tradition and a son receiving and staying with it), what you have is called an אבן *(even)* – a stone – a merging of אב and בן. The Jewish nation is built from these units.

We build with stones!

When we visit the graves of parents or other family members who have passed away, the custom is to leave a small stone on the grave,[4] unlike people of other societies, who leave flowers.

Besides the fact that a stone does not wither quickly, the idea that we are conveying, by placing a stone, is that we understand what the one who passed away stood for and we are continuing on his path.

Now it is clear why Yosef received the blessing that he should be "a shepherd, a *stone* of Yisrael."[5]

---

4. *Be'er Heitev, O.H.* 224:8. He mentions a custom to place grass on the grave, which does wither. Today the prevalent custom is the placing of a stone.
5. Bereishis 49:24.

6.5 STONES ON THE SHOULDERS

Going back, it becomes clear why the image of Yaakov, when appearing to Yosef at the moment of temptation with Potiphar's wife, threatens him:

> *"Your brothers are destined to have their names engraved on the* ***stones of the ephod****, and your name is meant to be with them. Do you want your name to be effaced from being among them? You will be known as 'one who keeps company with harlots,' as it is written, 'one who keeps company with harlots will lose much wealth.'"*[6,7]

The *ephod*, one of the eight garments of the High Priest, had shoulder straps from which the breastplate was hung. On each shoulder strap was a precious stone. The command to make the *ephod* says:

> *Take two shoham*[8] *stones, and engrave on them the names of the* ***sons of Yisrael****.*[9] *There shall be six names on one stone, and the remaining six names on the other stone,*[10] *in the order of their birth.*[11]

---

6. Mishlei 29:3.
7. *Sota* 36b, quoted in section 5.3.
8. The identity of the *shoham* stones is a matter of discussion. The Targum translates the phrase as אבני בורלא, a cognate of "beryl." Others explain they were sardonyx stones.
9. A name of Yaakov – Bereishis 32:29.
10. These two stones, which contain the names of the twelve tribes, are not the only stones which have the names of the tribes engraved upon them. There were also the twelve stones of the *choshen*, the breastplate of the *Kohen Gadol*, one stone for each tribe.
    Why is the threat that Yosef's name will be effaced from the stones of the *ephod*, rather than losing his stone one the *choshen*?
    R. Yaakov Marcus, in his work on the tractate *Sotah*, *Minchas Yaakov*, explains:

If Yosef would have lost his connection with his father then the appropriate consequence would be no longer having his name on a stone of the *ephod*.[12] He would no longer have been part of the אבן, the building of continuity, of the Jewish People.

We now have a better understanding as to why stones play such a central role in the story of Yaakov and Lavan. An אבן, a stone, represents faithful continuity of a father's path. That was the essential struggle between them.

To summarize:

- The combination of father (אב) and son (בן) leads to אבן – a stone.

The two stones of the *ephod* are referred to as אבני זכרון, "stones of remembrance" (Shemos 28:12, 39:7). Rashi (on Shemos 28:12) explains the concept of remembrance regarding these stones: "That the Holy one, Blessed is He should see [the names of] the tribes written in front of Him, and He should remember their righteousness." That is the essence of these two stones. If Yosef sins with Potiphar's wife, it would be totally inappropriate for his name to appear on the stones that remind the Almighty of the righteousness of the tribes. The twelve stones of the *choshen*, however, are never referred to as "stones of remembrance."

Knowing this, it is interesting that Yosef is asked by the image of his father, "Your brothers are destined to have their names engraved on the stones of the *ephod*, and your name is meant to be with them. Do you want your name to be effaced from being *among them*?" On the *choshen* each brother had his own separate stone. On the *ephod* the names were *together*, six on each stone. So the phrase "from being among them" is especially apt.

It is fascinating to note that the word "stone" or "stones" occurs eleven times in the *parshah* of *Vayeitzei*, one time for each of the eleven sons of Yaakov born in the *parshah*. In the following *parshah*, there is only one mention of "stone." This is when Yaakov builds a pillar of "stone" in Beit-El (Bereishis 35:14), immediately prior to the birth of his twelfth son, Binyamin. Twelve stones for twelve sons!

11. Shemos 28:9-10.
12. It is intriguing that the prince of the tribe of Menashe, one of the sons of Yosef, who will represent his tribe in inheriting the land of Israel, is called "Chaniel, the son of *Ephod*" (Bamidbar 34:23).

- The relationships of fathers transmitting and sons receiving tradition are the building-blocks of the Jewish nation.
- We build with stones!
- It is the realization by Yosef that he will lose having his name on the stone of the *ephod* which enables him to remain connected to his tradition.

7

No son, no sons

7.1 LAVAN – NOT A SON

We have seen that אבן is contraction of אב and בן and thus represents continuity.

What about Lavan?

לָבָן is a contraction of לא בן, i.e., "not a son."[1] There is no more appropriate name for this man!

As we have seen, he has no relationship with his father[2] and tries to sever Yaakov's connection with Yitzchak.[3] His whole being is a struggle against the authority of fathers.

Stones are thus crucial to the story of Yaakov and Lavan. Yaakov knows he is threatened by Lavan (לא–בן), and, therefore, keeps a connection to stones (אבן). Yaakov is well aware that stones represent the continuity of the father-son tradition that he is destined to

---

1. This type of exegesis is found, for example, in *Nedarim* 11a - מאי לחולין – לא לחולין ליהוי אלא קרבן. An example from *midrash* is found in *Bereishis Rabbah* 24:5 – "ויאמר לאדם" – לא לאדם אני נותן כי אם לבניו.
2. See sections 2.1 and 2.3.
3. Section 2.4.

establish forever for the Jewish nation. He therefore uses stones wherever possible to emphasize his link to his father.

As we saw,[4] on the way to the home of Lavan:

> *He came to a certain place and spent the night there because the sun had already set. He took **stones** of that place and put them under his head and lay down to sleep there.*[5]

When he wakes

> *He takes the **stone** which he had placed under his head and erected it as a standing stone. He poured oil upon it.*[6]

Divine providence also helps emphasize the stone link by making stones an even greater part of Yaakov's story. On arrival, Yaakov sees a well.

> *The mouth of the well was covered with a large **stone**. When all the flocks were gathered there, they would roll the **stone** from the mouth of the well and water the sheep. Then they would replace the **stone** on the well's mouth in its place.*[7]

When Yaakov sees Rivkah coming to the well with her father's flock:

> *He rolls the **stone** from the mouth of the well and waters the sheep of Lavan, his mother's brother.*[8]

This episode contains the *only* mention, in the entire Tenach, of a *stone* as the cover of a well.

Why is the idea of a stone written here?

At a deeper level, before he can marry Rachel, who is the daughter of Lavan (לֹא–בֵן), Yaakov needs to ascertain whether she understands

---

4. Section 1.7.
5. Bereishis 28:11.
6. Ibid., v. 18.
7. Ibid., 29:2-3.
8. Ibid., v. 10.

the importance of connection between parents and children and, therefore, shows her a big stone (אבן).[9]

Twenty years later, before making a covenant with this dangerous man, Yaakov makes sure that both he and his sons have understood this concept.

> *Yaakov takes a* ***stone*** *and raises it as a pillar. Yaakov tells his brothers (sons): "Collect* ***stones.****" They take* ***stones*** *and make a pile.*[10]

7.2 LAVAN – NO SONS

Since Lavan is the antithesis of father-son relationships, it is not surprising to read the following comment of Rashi. Lavan is trying to persuade Yaakov to stay longer after working fourteen years for Rachel and Leah.

> *Lavan said to him, "If I have found favor in your eyes, I have used divination and know that Hashem has blessed me because of you."*[11]

What is the blessing which Lavan has received?
Rashi clarifies:

> *"I have used divination" – "I was a diviner; I ascertained through my divining that blessing came to me as a result of you. When you arrived here* ***I did not have sons,****" as it says, "Behold, Rachel, his daughter, is coming with the flock."*[12] *Is it possible that he had sons and sends his daughters to work with*

---

9. In view of this idea, there is something appropriate about the prevalent custom to give an engagement ring which has a precious stone – to convey the message that continuity and connection to tradition are crucial.
10. Bereishis 31:45-46.
11. Ibid., 30.27.
12. Ibid., 29:6.

> *the shepherds? Now he has sons, as it says, "He heard the words of Lavan's sons."*[13]

Not only is Lavan (לא-בן) not a son, but on his own, he was incapable of having sons! Not only can לא בן mean "not a son," but it also means "has no son."

It is only in the merit of Yaakov, who is constantly yearning to be back in his father's home,[14] that Lavan has sons!

7.3 HOW MANY BROTHERS DOES YAAKOV HAVE?

It is intriguing to examine the construction of the pile of stones used to make a covenant between Yaakov and Lavan:

> *Yaakov took a stone and raised it as a pillar. Yaakov told his brothers: "Collect stones." They took stones and made a pile.*[15]

Firstly, who are the "brothers" of Yaakov? He only has one brother, Esav, who is not in the vicinity!

Rashi answers the question:

> *"His brothers" – They are his sons, who are like brothers to him, coming close to him in times of trouble and war.*

In other words, they are sons who are unified with their father, fighting together as brothers-in-arms.

A few verses later, Yaakov prepares a meal:

> *Yaakov slaughtered a sacrifice on the mountain and called his brothers to eat bread.*[16]

Who are "his brothers"?

---

13. Ibid., 31:1.
14. See section 2.2.
15. Bereishis 31:45-46.
16. Ibid., v. 54.

There is no reason he would be making a feast for his sons.[17] So Rashi clarifies:

> *"For his brothers" – The friends who were with Lavan.*

In other words, the phrase "his brothers" refers to Lavan and not Yaakov.

Although Lavan has sons, they are not one with their father. As such, the phrase can only mean "friends." He has sons, but there is no relationship of unity with them.

Even more condemning is what the Torah reveals to us about his relationship with his daughters, Rachel and Leah.

After Hashem appears to Yaakov and tells him to return to the land of his fathers, Yaakov tells his wives.

> *Yaakov sent word and summoned Rachel and Leah to the field where his flock was.*[18]

The Midrash[19] asks why they spoke in the field, rather than in their house.

Rashi answers the question:

> *"Only in a field" – As people say, "The walls have ears."*

We see clearly that Yaakov and his wives felt that Lavan was not to be trusted and all discussions had to be kept secret.

When Yaakov tells his wives that Hashem appeared to him and told him to return home, what is their reaction?

---

17. See *Sifsei Chachamim,* ad loc. He asks why the use of the word "brothers" earlier, "Yaakov told his brothers: 'Collect stones,'" (Bereishis 31:46), does not also refer to the friends of Lavan. The answers given is that Yaakov would not use the imperative form לקטו, "collect," with people who were not obliged to obey him, whereas with his sons this form would be totally appropriate.
18. Bereishis 31:4.
19. *Midrash Tanchuma Hakadum, Vayeitzei.*

Rachel and Leah answered and said to him, "Do we still have any portion or inheritance in our father's home? He considers us strangers, for he sold us and consumed our money!"[20]

This is probably the most damning indictment of any father in the Torah. We have a father who, according to the testimony of our righteous mothers, treats his daughters as total strangers. He sells them in marriage, and does not give them a penny!

Not only is he a man who destroys connection between fathers and sons, but he has no connection with daughters, either.

7.4 "HE DOESN'T HELP AT ALL!"

Let us return to Yaakov's "brothers," i.e., sons, who built the pile of stones. How old were they?

We can work it out. Yaakov worked seven years for Rachel. Then he married Leah and Rachel. After that he worked another seven years for Rachel. He then worked six years, in return for certain types of sheep and goats. In total, twenty years. As he says to Lavan,

"Twenty years I have been with you!"[21]

He originally wanted to return after the first fourteen years, after the birth of Yosef:

After Rachel had given birth to Yosef, Yaakov said to Lavan, "Let me leave, that I can go to my place and my land."[22]

That means that Reuven, the oldest son, could not be older than twelve years old,[23] and Yosef, the youngest, was a mere six years old.

20. Bereishis 31:14-15.
21. Ibid., v. 38.
22. Ibid., 30:25.
23. Yaakov married Leah after seven years with Lavan. Assuming nine months until the birth of Reuven, he would be twelve and a quarter at the end of the twenty-year stay.

These young boys are the ones who are carrying the boulders to make the pile.

Neither Lavan, nor the friends with him, lift a finger to help the youngsters. There is total lack of interest on the part of Lavan in helping his grandchildren. There is no unity with sons - nor with grandsons![24]

Insult is added to injury when Lavan announces to Yaakov,

> *"Here is this pile and here is this pillar* ***which I have erected*** *between me and you."*[25]

He did not touch a stone!

In fact, Lavan (לא–בן) is incapable of touching a stone (אבן).

7.5 A DONKEY DIALOGUE

It is fascinating to see this same theme of inability to father children in the story of Bilam.

We saw that Bilam rode his donkey to go and curse the Jewish people. The angel blocked his path three times to symbolize the three fathers that Bilam was trying to disconnect from the Jews.[26]

When Bilam's donkey is blocked by the angel the third time, Bilam hits the donkey with a staff.[27] The donkey speaks to Bilam:

---

24. Why then is he called "Lavan ben Nachor" (Bereishis 29:5), implying a connection to his *grandfather*? Yaakov uses this name because he has to designate which Lavan he is talking about and this name still indicates a disconnection from his father. Here we see that, in actuality, Lavan is not interested in offering any help to his grandchildren.
25. Bereishis 31:51. The *Torah Shlemah* (Kasher) on this verse adduces a *midrash* which points out that it was not Lavan who erected the pile. Why should he claim to have done something that he did not do? Perhaps he is even more dangerous if his real intent is not overt. His total opposition to all that stones represent is not openly revealed.
26. Section 3.8.
27. The first two times there is no mention of a staff.

"Am I not your donkey, upon which you have ridden your entire life? Have I ever been in the habit of doing this?"[28]

Chazal interpret this as one side of a three way conversation:

[The ministers of Moav who accompanied Bilam] said to him, "What is the reason you are not riding a horse?"[29]
"I sent it out to graze in moist pasture."
*"**Am I not your donkey**?" [the donkey asked, implying that Bilam always used her.]*
"Merely for carrying." [Bilam tried to explain the comment of the donkey in a way which will not prove him to be a liar.]
*"**Upon which you have ridden**."*
"Only occasionally."
*"**Your entire life.** Furthermore, I provide you with cohabitation at night."*
The proof to this is that the donkey said, "Have I ever been in the habit" – ההסכן הסכנתי. This phrase has a similar root to the phrase ותהי לו סכנת,[30] *where the connotation is of a woman lying with a man.*[31]

Bilam rode the donkey rather than a horse because he also uses it for immoral purposes. No children will be born. Bilam is also לא בן!

7.6 KILL ALL THE SONS

If we see that a person in Torah has a certain approach or feature of character, we can expect to find it in several episodes

28. Bamidbar 22:30.
29. A horse is far more appropriate for an important personage like Bilam than a donkey.
30. I Melachim 1:2. The verse is talking about the young woman who would lie with King David, in his old age, to keep his body warm.
31. *Sanhedrin* 105b.

where this person appears.

For example, it is fascinating to see how, in *every* appearance of Avimelech, king of the Pelishtim, he always refuses to take the blame for his actions. This is true both in his dealings with Avraham and with Yitzchak.[32]

Having seen that Bilam attempts to prevent connection between fathers and sons, it is illuminating to study an earlier episode in his life, which occurred when the Jews were in Egypt.

> *The children of Israel were fruitful, teemed, multiplied and became exceedingly strong; the land was filled with them.*
> *A new king arose in Egypt who did not know of Yosef. He said to his people, "Behold, the populace of the children of Israel are more numerous and stronger than we are. Let us deal wisely with it, lest it increase in numbers and it may be that if a war occurs, it, too, may join our enemies, wage war against us, driving [us] from the land."*[33]

Having tried slave labor, and after an unsuccessful attempt to have the midwives kill the Jewish baby boys immediately upon birth, Pharaoh tries a different tactic:

> *Pharaoh commanded his entire people, saying, "Every son that will be born you will cast into the river, and every daughter you shall keep alive."*[34]

Who advised Pharaoh to use this stratagem? Our Sages reveal the identity:

> *"Let us deal wisely with it [the Jewish people]"*[35] *– Rabbi Chiya bar Abba taught in the name of Rabbi Simmai: "There were*

---

32. See Bereishis 20:4-5, 9; 21:26; 26:9-10, 27-29.
33. Shemos 1:7-10.
34. Ibid., v. 22
35. Ibid., v. 10.

> *three involved in the plot*[36] *– Bilam, Iyov and Yisro.*
> *Bilam who advised [killing the sons] was killed [by the Jews in the war against Midian*[37]*].*
> *Iyov, who remained silent, was condemned to suffer.*
> *Yisro, who fled, merited that his descendants would sit in the Chamber of hewn-stone [as members of the Sanhedrin, the ultimate authority of Jewish law]."*[38]

Each of the three advisers is treated "measure for measure":

Bilam, who tries to kill, is killed.

Iyov, who is insensitive to the suffering that will be inflicted, is punished with suffering.

Yisro, who forgoes his position as adviser to Pharaoh to avoid complicity in such cruelty, is rewarded with descendants who will advise and guide the Jewish nation.

It is totally in character that Bilam, the arch-opponent of the father-son relationship, should be the one who suggests killing all the sons.

However, this is not the full extent of his evil plan.

> *Pharaoh commanded his entire people, saying, "Every son that will be born you will cast into the river, and* ***every daughter you shall keep alive.****"*[39]

If only the boys were to be killed, then by definition the girls will remain alive. Why is there a need to say "and every daughter you shall keep alive"?

Our Rabbis answer:

---

36. This teaching is based upon the idea that "Let us deal wisely with it" is connected with the decree to throw the sons into the river Nile.
37. See section 4.1-4.2.
38. *Sotah* 11a, *Sanhedrin* 106a.
39. Shemos 1:22.

> *Why did Pharaoh need to keep the females alive? Since the Egyptians were immersed in immorality they said, "Let us kill the males and keep the females as our women."*[40]

Not only does Bilam want to kill the sons, but he also tries to taint the sanctity of the Jewish nation with immorality. This behavior will repeat itself when the Jews have left Egypt and are in the wilderness. We saw how Bilam tries to cut the connection between fathers and sons[41] and attempts to sully the sanctity of the Jewish nation by means of seduction by the Midianite women.[42] This line of attack was already evident in Egypt. Once again, we see the two lines of attack, striking at the continuity and sanctity of the Jewish People.

7.7 BUILDING BALAK

When Bilam is about to attempt to curse the Jews, he requests seven altars to counter the seven altars built by Avraham, Yitzchak and Yaakov.[43]

> *Bilam said to Balak, "**Build me** seven altars here, and prepare me seven bulls and seven rams."*
> *Balak did as Bilam had said. Balak and Bilam offered up a bull and a ram on each altar. Bilam said to Balak, "Stand by your burnt offering, and I will go. Perhaps Hashem will come to meet me. Whatever He shows me I will tell you." He went off alone.*
> *G-d happened upon Bilam. He [Bilam] said to Him [G-d], "**I have set up** the seven altars and I have offered up a bull and a ram on each altar."*[44]

---

40. *Shemos Rabbah* 1:18.
41. See chapter 3.
42. See section 3.6.
43. See section 3.9.
44. Bamidbar 23:1-4.

Once again, Bilam, alias Lavan (לא–בן), does not touch a stone. Balak does the building, and yet Bilam, like Lavan, takes the credit – "I have set up the seven altars."[45]

7.8 "DON'T HAVE SONS!"

We have seen that Lavan has no connection with his father,[46] and that he tries to disconnect Yaakov from his father.[47]

We also have learnt that Lavan, in his own right, is incapable of having sons.[48] It should be no surprise to see that Lavan tries to prevent Yaakov from having sons.

Firstly, Yaakov, who was already seventy-seven years old when he comes to Lavan,[49] is made to wait seven years until he can marry. Lavan does not give him his daughter straight away.

---

45. We find the same the third time Bilam tries to curse: "Bilam said to Balak, 'Build me seven altars here, and prepare me seven bulls and seven rams.'" (Bamidbar 23:29) This verse is identical to Bamidbar 23:1, (besides one less *yud* in the Hebrew word for "rams," אילם in place of אילים).
   The second time Bilam goes to curse, there is a slight ambiguity.
   "He [Balak] took him to a field with a view and he built seven altars and offered up a bull and ram on each altar. He said to Balak, 'Stand here by your burnt offering, while I go to the meeting there.'" (Bamidbar 23:14-15)
   Who built the altars? We can infer that it was Balak for a number of reasons. Firstly, he built them the first and third time and so it is reasonable to assume that he built them the second time as well. Secondly, he is the subject of the first phrase, "He [Balak] took him to a field" and, therefore, is presumably the subject of "and he built."
   Thirdly, and most conclusively, the one who built the altars is the one who offered up the sacrifices, the subject being the same. Bilam says to Balak, "Stand here by *your* burnt offering." Balak is the one who brought the offerings, and is, therefore, the one who built the altars.
46. Sections 2.1 and 2.3.
47. Section 2.4 and 5.1.
48. Section 7.2
49. See Rashi on Bereishis 28:9. Yosef is born at the end of fourteen years of work, and is thirty years old when he appears in front of Pharaoh. Yaakov stands in front of Pharaoh after seven years of plenty and two years of

At the end of the seven years,

Yaakov said to Lavan, "Give me my wife, for the years are fulfilled, that I may come (ואבואה) *to her."*[50]

The phrase "that I may come to her" is a euphemism for marital relations.[51] Rashi answers the question of how a man of the stature of Yaakov could say such a phrase.

"For the years are fulfilled" – "...I am already eighty-four years old.[52] *When will I establish twelve tribes?"*
That is the meaning of "that I may come to her," because not even the most light-headed person would use such a phrase. The intention here is only to give birth to children.

Yaakov has no thoughts of personal, physical pleasure, but only to fulfill his spiritual destiny. He is fully aware that Lavan will again try to thwart him, preventing him from having children and building the Jewish People. Yaakov is therefore insistent that he should receive his wife at once.

As we know, Lavan succeeds in giving Yaakov a different wife than the one agreed – he marries Leah in place of Rachel.

Divine providence, however, ensures that this is only for the best. Why? Yaakov needed children in order to begin building the Jewish nation. At this time, Rachel *could not* be his wife because she was physically incapable of bearing children!

---

famine, by which time Yosef is thirty-nine years old. Yaakov tells Pharaoh that he is one hundred and thirty years old. So we can compute the age at which Yaakov arrived at the home of Lavan: 130-14-30-9=77.

50. Bereishis 29:21.
51. See, for example the first *mishnah* of tractate *Kiddushin*, which discusses how a woman is acquired in marriage and says, נקנית בכסף בשטר ובביאה, meaning "she is acquired with money, or a document or marital relations."
52. Rashi is interpreting the phrase "for the years are fulfilled," not as referring to the seven years that Yaakov had agreed to work, but to the years of his life, i.e., "I am already an old man."

What changed? In what merit does Rachel miraculously have a child? Our Rabbis reveal:

> *"And G-d remembered Rachel. [G-d heard her and He opened her womb.]" – What did He remember? Her silence concerning her sister. When Leah was given in her stead, Rachel knew, and still remained silent.*[53]

Were Lavan not to have deceived Yaakov, Rachel would never have had children! Fortunately, he was not aware of the future consequences of his actions.[54]

7.9 LAVAN – THE LIAR WITH THE LYRE

Not only does Lavan want to prevent Yaakov from producing sons, but even after they are born, he wants to seize them from Yaakov.

Lavan pursues Yaakov and his family, who have fled from him. When he catches up with Yaakov, he says with righteous indignation:

> *"What have you done? You deceived me and led my daughters away, like prisoners of war! Why did you leave so secretly? You deceived me and told me nothing. I would have sent you off with celebration and song, with drum and lyre. You did not even let me kiss my sons and daughters [farewell]."*[55]

---

53. *Bereishis Rabbah* 73:4
54. How can it be that Rachel would never have had children without Lavan's deception? Was she not destined to be one of the Matriarchs? The answer is that the Almighty *knew* that that this deception would take place and how Rachel would respond.
    This idea is found many times in the Torah. For example, the Almighty had *promised* Avraham that He would enslave and redeem his descendants. Yet we read, "G-d heard their cry and He remembered the covenant with Avraham, Yitzchak and Yaakov." (Shemos 2:24) The clear implication is that it is only because of the "cry" that He remembers the covenant and redeems the Jews. The answer is that the Almighty *knew* that they would cry.
55. Bereishis 31:26-28.

It is laughable to read these sentiments. We can only begin to imagine what Rachel and Leah were thinking, listening to this. We already know what they had to say about Lavan.[56]

7.10 "ALL OF YOU!"

Perhaps the most spine-chilling words in the story are the next words of Lavan:

> *"You acted stupidly. I have the power to do you great harm, but your father's G-d spoke to me last night and said, 'Be careful not to say anything, good or bad, to Yaakov.'"*[57]

The clear implication is that were G-d not to have appeared to Lavan, he *would* have done harm. To whom?

In modern English, the word "you" is used for both singular and plural.

In old English there is the distinction between "thou," which is singular, and "you," which is plural. Similarly, French has "tu" and "vous," and German has "du" and "sie."

Hebrew also has different expressions for singular and plural. It is important to see which is used.

Let us look carefully at what Lavan said:

> *"I have the power to do **you** great harm."*

The Hebrew is: יש לאל ידי לעשות **עמכם** רע.

The word **עמכם** means the plural "you."[58] In other words, Lavan would have harmed not only Yaakov his son-in-law, but also his daughters and grandsons. Terrifying!

---

56. Section 7.3.
57. Bereishis 31:28-29.
58. Or, as a Texan student of mine once put it, "Y'all!"

7.11 "IT'S ALL MINE!"

To see the full extent of Lavan's egocentricity and megalomania, we need to look at what he says immediately before he makes the covenant with Yaakov:

> *"The daughters are my daughters! The sons are my sons! The flocks are my flocks! Everything you see is mine!"*[59]

If it was up to Lavan, Yaakov would have had nothing! Lavan wanted Yaakov to have no sons. [60]

7.12 IDOL PURSUIT

When Yaakov takes his family and possessions and flees from the home of Lavan, Lavan pursues them. On catching up with them, he says to Yaakov,

> *"Why did you steal my gods?"*[61]

---

59. Bereishis 31:43.
60. If Lavan is talking about "the sons" from the standpoint of their relationship to Yaakov, what about the phrase "daughters"? They cannot be the daughters of Yaakov, since, according to the straightforward reading of the story, Yaakov had only one daughter, and, furthermore, "the daughters" would not be mentioned before "the sons." Therefore, they must be the daughters of Lavan himself!? They are the wives of Yaakov! If so, there is inconsistency between the phrases "sons" and "daughters," the first being from the perspective of Yaakov, whereas the second is from the perspective of Lavan. The answer is that Lavan cannot refer to his daughters as "wives," but he can refer to grandsons as "sons," following the principle בני בנים הרי הן כבנים – "Grandchildren are considered children" (*Yevamos* 62b). Now the phrase "sons" has two meanings: "The sons" means the sons of Yaakov; "my sons" means grandchildren. Interestingly, the Talmud attempts to derive the principle from this statement of Lavan, i.e., "your sons are considered like my sons," but rejects the attempt because of the phrase "the flocks are my flocks." The phrase "my sons" there is understood to mean "sons acquired through me."
61. Bereishis 31:30.

Indeed, his idols *were* stolen. Who had taken them?

> *Rachel stole the idols (terafim) belonging to her father.*[62]

Why should she want to do such a thing? Rashi answers the question:

> *"Rachel stole the idols" – She intended to disconnect her father from idolatory.*

She is diametrically opposed to her father's way of life. Not only will she not follow it, she will do her utmost to stop him following it!

Where does she hide them?

> *Rachel had taken the idols, had put them in the cushion of a camel, and was sitting on them.*[63]

What could express her total disdain for her father's "precious" idols more than sitting on them?

Here is the result of a child rejecting the "tradition" of her father – but not the way Lavan had intended!

We have seen:

- The Almighty takes evil actions and makes them turn out for the best.[64]
- Lavan struggles against tradition, the family unit, and the authority of parents. He wants to ensure that children are disconnected from their parents, following a totally different path.
- The Almighty laughs and says, "If that is what you want, I will make it happen – but I do not think that you will like it!"
- Lavan's own daughters completely disconnect from him and become the building blocks (or, perhaps better,

---

62. Ibid., v. 19.
63. Ibid., v.34.
64. As we have seen in Section 7.7.

stones) of the Jewish People. To make it worse, Rachel tries to disconnect him from his idolatry by stealing his idols – and sitting on them!

7.13 NOT FOLLOWING LIKE SHEEP

Another astonishing example of how Lavan's agenda is used against him occurs with the sheep and goats which Yaakov receives for the six years he worked for Lavan, after the fourteen he worked for his wives.

Lavan tries to persuade Yaakov to continue working for him:

> *"What shall I give you?"*
> *Yaakov replied, "You shall give me nothing. Just do this one thing for me and I will come back to tend and guard your flock. I will pass through your entire flock today, removing every lamb that is spotted or streaked, all the brown ones from the sheep and all streaked or spotted goats. It is [those kinds] which will be my payment. In the future, this will be a sign of my integrity: You can examine anything I have taken as pay. Any goat that is not spotted or streaked, or any sheep that is not brown, can be considered stolen."*
> *Lavan said, "If only it will be according to your words."*
> *That day he [Lavan] removed the ringed and streaked he-goats, and all the spotted and streaked she-goats, and every one that had some white in it, and all the brown ones from the sheep. He gave them to his sons.*
> *He separated himself from Yaakov with the distance of a three day journey. Yaakov was left tending the rest of Lavan's flock.*[65]

Let us examine the agreement and see what type of animals Yaakov will receive as payment? Rashi elucidates:

---

65. Bereishis 30:31-36.

> *"Will be my payment" – Those born subsequently, which are spotted and streaked of the goats, and dark of the sheep, will be mine. Remove those types that are there now and deposit them with your sons so that you will not be able to claim that those born subsequently were already there initially. In addition, you will not be able to claim that because the males were spotted and streaked, the females gave birth to offspring which resembled them.*[66]

Yaakov is given no males of the types that it has been agreed that he will receive as payment.

What would happen if the children resemble their fathers? Yaakov will not receive one animal!

Lavan's struggle with Yaakov is based on the idea that he wants children to differ from their fathers. The Almighty has the last laugh. He arranges that this will happen with the sheep and goats, and the result is that Yaakov becomes fabulously wealthy.[67] Not exactly what Lavan had in mind when he made his agreement with Yaakov!

The irony is wonderful:

- Lavan tries to ensure that sons do not follow their fathers.
- The Almighty treats Lavan "measure for measure" and has Lavan's sheep and goats differing from their white parents.
- As a result, Yaakov receives all of Lavan's wealth.
- Lavan's own approach is used to create his downfall.

---

66. Rashi on Bereishis 30:32.
67. Bereishis 31:43.

8

Of towers and pyramids

8.1 THE TOWER OF BAVEL

Knowing the significance of אבן and its converse, לבן (לא בן), we can appreciate other sections of the Torah with a new depth of understanding.

One of the most famous episodes in the book of Bereishis is the story of the tower of Bavel.

What was the agenda of those who built the tower? The story starts as follows:

> *The entire earth had one language with uniform words.*[1]

The Hebrew for "uniform words" is דְּבָרִים אֲחָדִים, a very unusual phrase. The word אחד means "one." The Midrash explains what these דברים אחדים were:

> *Rebbe Yochanan*[2] *expounded:* דברים אחדים *means... sharp* (חדים)

---

1. Bereishis 11:1. Our translation is based on understanding the word אחדים as related to the word אחד meaning "one."

> *words against "Hashem our G-d, Hashem who is **One**,"*[3] *and against "Avraham, who was **one** in the land."*[4,5]
> *Against Avraham, they said, "He is a barren mule, who does not give birth."*[6]
> *Against "Hashem our G-d" they said, "It is not up to Him to choose the higher worlds for Himself and to give us the lower worlds. Let us construct a tower and make an idol on the top. We will place a sword in its hand and it will seem as if it is doing battle with Him."*[7]

What is the common denominator here between G-d and Avraham?

They are both fathers.

G-d is אבינו מלכנו, our Father our King.

Avraham is the first of our forefathers. He was originally called אברם, a contraction of אב ארם, "father of Aram," where he came from. His name was changed to אברהם, a contraction of אב המון, meaning

---

2. Our translation, writing that Rebbe Yochanan is the teacher of this idea, follows the understanding of the commentary *Eitz Yosef* and the notes of the Reshash.
3. Devarim 6:4. This is from the first verse of the *Shema* prayer.
4. The commentary of the Maharzu points out, based on the *Yalkut*, that the phrase "in the land" is out of place here. The reason is that the verse adduced, Yechezkel 33.24, actually says: אחד היה אברהם ויירש את הארץ. The translation of this verse would be "Avraham was one, and he inherited the land."
5. Rebbe Yochanan understands אחדים in two different ways: both as "sharp" (חדים) and as related to the word meaning "one," i.e., against those who are referred to as "one."
6. See *Eitz Yosef* who explains that they were saying that Avraham and his teaching of monotheism will have no continuity, since he has no children to perpetuate his beliefs.
7. *Bereishis Rabbah* 38:6.

"father of many (nations)."[8] He is the first man to have the word אב as part of his name, describing his essence as a father.[9]

The builders of the tower were not simply rebelling against G-d. While true, that does not explain the whole story. There would be no need to mention Avraham then. In reality, they were rebelling against the idea of "fathers and sons." They mocked Avraham's essence as a father by saying, *"He is a barren mule, who does not give birth,"* i.e., he is not even a real father.[10]

As opposed to Avraham, they did not accept G-d as their Father and superior. The Talmud, in listing the obligations a son has towards his father, includes:

> *One does not stand in his (father's) place, nor does one sit in his place.*[11]

They wanted to be in their Father's place, in the upper worlds. Like Lavan, they were rebelling against the very idea of fathers.

The fact that the entire scheme was one of rebellion, is highlighted by the fact the leader of the project was the king, Nimrod (נמרוד),[12] whose name means "let us rebel."

---

8. See Rashi on Bereishis 17:5. Rashi explains that according to the new name the letter *reish* does not fit, but since it was originally part of his name it was not removed when the name was changed.
9. He has a contemporary called אבימלך (see Bereishis 20:2), but in that case it is not Avimelech who is described as a father, but his father, i.e., it is Avimelech saying, "My father is king." The same is true regarding Avimael (ibid., 10:28).
10. Avraham was born in the year 1948 (from the creation of the world). This can be calculated by summing the years at which each of the generations from Adam until Terach, father of Avraham, gave birth. The tower of Bavel was built in the year 1996. Rashi (on Bereishis 10:25) demonstrates this in the light of the fact that this occurred in the last year of the life of Peleg. If so, Avraham was forty-eight years old at the time of the building of the tower. His first son, Yishmael, was not to be born for another thirty-eight years (see Bereishis 17:24-25).
11. *Kiddushin* 31b.

8.2 THE SAME WORD HERE AND THERE

A crucial tool for exegetic derivations of Torah laws is the *gezeirah shavah*. This is the second of the thirteen hermeneutical principles listed by Rebbe Yishmael.[13]

The principle is that if the same, or similar, words are found in two places in the Torah, then we can infer from one place to the other. This is a halachic principle, and is used to derive laws of one section from another. It can be used if there is a tradition from Sinai that the pair of words can be used in such a way.

A similar method of derivation is also used in the area of aggadic interpretation. If identical words occur in different sections of Torah, one can shed light on the other. One of the major exponents of this approach is the *Baal Haturim*, son of the Rosh.

Let us examine how the *Baal Haturim* uses this methodology to shed light on this section of Torah.

> ודברים אחדים –*The word* ודברים *occurs only twice in Tanach, here and Koheles (5:6), "matters of worthlessness and many words"* (ודברים הרבה)*. This teaches us that they (those who built the tower) spoke many matters of worthlessness (i.e., their mockery of the Almighty and of Avraham).*

The Baal Haturim speaks only of ודברים. He does not discuss where we find the second word of the phrase, אחדים. It is fascinating to see where else this word occurs.

The word אחדים is used to imply a disconnection from fathers. This idea is inherent in the word itself. The root is אחד, meaning "one." So אחדים, the plural, means a "number of ones," i.e., separate units, not connected.

---

12. See Rashi, Bereishis 10:11.
13. This list is included in morning prayers and is found in the *siddur*. It is printed at the end of tractate *Berachos* [Vilna], with elucidation.

There are only two other occurrences of the word in Chumash, both in the same context.

When Rivkah sends Yaakov to her brother Lavan (to flee from Esav), she says,

> *"Remain with him (Lavan) a few days* (ימים אחדים) *until your brother's fury has subsided."*[14]

Yaakov offered Lavan to work for seven years in exchange for receiving Rachel as a wife:

> *Yaakov loved Rachel and he said, "I will work seven years for Rachel, your younger daughter.*[15]

The years of work are described as follows:

> *Yaakov worked seven years for Rachel. He loved her so much, it seemed no more than a few days* (ימים אחדים).[16]

Rashi comments:

> *"I will work seven years" – These are the few days* (ימים אחדים) *which his mother had mentioned, "Remain with him (Lavan) a few days* (ימים אחדים)*."*[17] *The proof that this is so is that it is written "it seemed no more than a few days* (ימים אחדים)*."*

Note that both of these usages of the word אחדים refer to the period of separation between Yaakov and his parents. As with the Tower of Bavel, we see that אחדים connotes disconnection from parents.

In all of Tanach, there is only one other occurrence of the word אחדים. This is in the book of Daniel:

---

14. Bereishis 27:44.
15. Ibid., 29:18
16. Ibid., v. 20
17. Ibid., 27:44.

"...within a few days (ובימים אחדים) he shall be broken."[18]

This is referring to a king. There is ambiguity as to which king is being described, but the use of the phrase ובימים אחדים is clear, as Rashi explains:

"Within a few days (ובימים אחדים) he shall be broken" – Within a few days his kingship shall be broken.

In other words, there will be no continuity. The sons will not inherit their father's position.

Every time the word אחדים is used is it in the context of separation or discontinuity from parents! It is the very opposite of אבן, the connection between אב and בן!

8.3 ANOTHER BRICK IN THE WALL

It is intriguing to see what is used to build the tower:

They said to one another, "Come, let us make bricks (לבנים) and fire them." They had brick (הלבנה) as stone (לאבן).[19]

They are not using stones, אבנים *(avanim)*, which connote a connection between sons and fathers *(av* and *ben)*; they are using bricks, לבנים *(levenim)*, implying no connection – לא בנים *(lo banim)*, no sons.

If we value life, we respect those who bestowed it upon us (parents). Conversely, where there is no respect for parents, there is no respect for the sanctity of human life.

With this in mind, we can appreciate the following Midrash:

When, in the course of construction, a man would fall off the building and die, they would not pay any attention. However, if

---

18. Daniel 11:20.
19. Bereishis 11:3.

> *a brick would drop, they would sit and cry and say, "When will another brick be brought in its place?"*[20]

There is a great difference between a stone and a brick. A stone is a solid piece of material, unchanging and a symbol of continuity. A brick is made from clay that has been hardened. Bricks disintegrate, stones do not.[21] The builders of the Tower did not use אבנים. They were not connected to previous generations, and they had no respect for parents. Life itself, then, was not valued.

Not only does the use of bricks represent a rejection of the relationship with parents, but also a rejection of the Almighty.

R. Samson Raphael Hirsch, in explaining why they used bricks, rather than stones, writes:

> *They found a plain that was lacking in all building material, but they wished to remain there. "Let us see if we can manufacture something ourselves, let us manufacture artificial stones," they said.*
> *Man discovers his own power and becomes proud of the artificial means at his disposal. He thinks that the community is exempt from serving G-d and from observing the laws of morality. "The ancients had to have stones, but we are able to build even where there are no stones."*

Just as we saw that the tower of Bavel was an expression of rebellion against Avraham, the representation of fatherhood, and against the Almighty, so too the material used represents this double rebellion!

---

20. *Pirkei D'Rebbe Eliezer*, ch.24.
21. This idea has halachic significance regarding laws of ritual purity. See *Niddah* 27b.

The struggle between the rebellion of Nimrod and the connection of Avraham comes to a climax when Nimrod tries to kill Avraham. How does he attempt this? Rashi enlightens us:

> *Terach complained to Nimrod that his son, Avraham, had destroyed his idols. Nimrod had him cast into a fiery* ***furnace.***[22]

Why a furnace?

We have seen that Nimrod was using bricks and not stones:

> *They said to one another, "Come, let us make bricks* (לבנים) *and fire them." They had brick* (הלבנה) *as stone* (לאבן).[23]

Rashi's comment on this verse completes the picture:

> *"And fire them" – That is how one makes bricks* (לבנים)*, which are called "tiules" (in old French)*[24] *– one fires them in a* ***furnace****.*

Nimrod is the one who rebels against G-d and the tradition and authority of fathers. He tries to kill Avraham, who is the exponent of father-son relationships. He does so in a furnace, because that is where they make לבנים – which themselves symbolize everything Nimrod is fighting for!

What could be more appropriate?

One last thought:

Although the builders of the tower were "one family," speaking one language, the inevitable result of building with bricks, rather than stones, is:

> *Hashem dispersed them across the entire face of the Earth, and they ceased building the city.*[25]

---

22. Rashi on Bereishis 11:28.
23. Bereishis 11:3.
24. "Tiles" in English.
25. Bereishis 11:8.

The consequence of rebelling against the father-son bond is that they are no longer one family, physically dispersed and disunited in language.

It is remarkable to see the link between the rebellion of Bavel and Lavan. The Torah describes the empire of Nimrod:

> *The beginning of his kingdom was Bavel, Erech, Accad, and Calneh, in the land of Shinar.*[26]

Where are these places *"Erech, Accad, and Calneh"*?

The Yalkut Shimoni informs us:

> *They are **Aram**, Netzivin and Ketifin.*[27]

Aram is the country of Lavan.

The *Midrash Rabbah* goes further:

> *"Erech, Accad, and Calneh" are **Charan**, Netzivin and Ketifin.*[28]

Charan is the *town* of Lavan![29]

How appropriate that Lavan is part of the empire of Nimrod!

It is really remarkable:

- Nimrod initiates the project of building the tower of Bavel as a rebellion against all that fathers represent.
- This was an attack against both the Almighty, our Divine Father, and Avraham, whose name and essence signifies fatherhood.
- Therefore, it is not **אבנים**, stones, which are used since they represent connection between fathers and sons.

---

26. Ibid., 10:10.
27. *Yalkut Shimoni, Bereishis remez* 62.
28. *Bereishis Rabbah* 37:4.
29. See section 2.3.

- It is לבנים, bricks, which are the material of construction. These represent disconnection between fathers and sons – לא–בנים.
- It is fascinating that Lavan, who shares this approach, lives in the empire of Nimrod.

8.4 HOW THE PYRAMIDS WERE BUILT

Another episode which can now be appreciated in a far more profound manner is the subjugation of the Jews in Egypt.

Pharaoh tries to prevent the increase in numbers and power of the Jews, using several stratagems:

> *The Egyptians made the children of Israel do body-breaking work. They made their lives miserable with hard labor, involving mortar and* ***bricks*** (לבנים).[30]

The Egyptians' plan is that if the Jews are forced to work with לבנים, rather than אבנים, then their continuity can be destroyed.

Our Rabbis reveal to what extent this plan reaches:

> *[If] any man was lacking one brick* (לבנה) *[from his daily quota], the Egyptians forcibly took his young boy... and placed him in the building in place of the brick.*[31]

Here we have the idea of לבנים (bricks) destroying בנים (sons) in its most powerful form!

However, this plan is miraculously foiled by the Almighty:

> *The more they (the Egyptians) afflicted them, the more they (the Jews) proliferated and spread.*[32]

Pharaoh's next tactic is to murder the Jewish boys at birth:

---

30. Shemos 1:13-14.
31. *Sefer Hayashar*, (Tel Aviv, 1955) pp. 188-189.
32. Shemos 1:12.

> *The king of Egypt spoke to the Hebrew midwives, whose names were Shifra and Puah. He said, "When you deliver Hebrew women, look upon the birthing stones* (הָאָבְנָיִם)*. If it is a son, kill him; but if it is a daughter, let her live."*[33]

Considering all we have learned, it is incredible: Pharaoh originally uses *levenim* to kill us. When this fails, where is the next battle for Jewish survival and continuity being fought? On the birthing *stones*! That is where sons are born – the place where the new generation comes into being, enabling אב to pass onto בן.

We have come full-circle when we remember what we saw in the previous chapter,[34] i.e., that Bilam was the adviser of Pharaoh! He is the one who suggested killing the sons!

Having seen the centrality of bricks (לבנים) in the subjugation by the Egyptians, it is remarkable to look at the song that the Jews sing when they are saved from the pursuing Egyptian army at the Reed Sea.[35] This song is known as שירת הים *(Shiras Hayam)* – the "Song of the Sea."

Occasionally the spaces between words in a section of a Torah scroll are of unusual length. This is sometimes so in Nach as well. This gives the section a distinctive appearance. The reason for the unusal spacing should be investigated.

There is a directive that *Shiras Hayam* should be written:

> אריח על גבי לבינה ולבינה על גבי אריח
>
> *Half brick on brick and brick on half brick.*[36]

---

33. Ibid., vv. 15-16.
34. Section 7.6.
35. Although ים סוף is often referred to as the "Red Sea," this is a misnomer. The literal translation is the "Sea of Reeds," and so it should be called the "Reed Sea."
36. *Maseches Soferim*, ch. 12 para.10

There is wide spacing between phrases, with phrases being written above spaces in the line below. The result is that the section looks like brickwork.

The song that that the Jewish nation sang expressed their awareness that everything that had happened to them in Egypt was all for their good. Thus the spacing is called אריח על גבי לבינה, echoing the לבנים (bricks) of slavery.

Therefore even the bricks which they had been forced to make become part of the song. Beautiful!

We have seen:

- Pharaoh tries to destroy Jewish continuity.
- He uses לבנים to achieve this end.
- The Jewish babies, which will ensure continuity, are born on הָאָבְנָיִם, the birthing-stones.
- It was Bilam, of all people, who advised Pharaoh to kill the Jewish baby boys. Again we see his attempt to destroy our continuity!

9

Why use their blessings?

9.1 A DANGEROUS BLESSING

Several chapters back, we raised a question:[1]

At two important occasions we use blessings of non-Jews. When we enter our synagogues in the morning, we say the blessing of Bilam:

מה טבו אהליך יעקב משכנתיך ישראל:

"How good are your tents, Yaakov, your tabernacles, Yisrael."[2]

This blessing alludes to "houses of prayer and study halls."[3] The relevance of the verse is clear. Nevertheless, why use the blessing of the evil Bilam, rather than a verse from Tehillim, authored by King David?

Similarly, there is a custom that when a Jewish couple are about to be married, the bridegroom covers the bride's face with a veil.[4] This

---

1. In section 3.11.
2. Bamidbar 24:5.
3. Section 3.4.
4. See *Kitzur Shulchan Aruch* 147:3.

ceremony is called *badeken*, from the Yiddish meaning "covering." The bystanders bless the bride:

> אחתנו את היי לאלפי רבבה ויירש זרעך את שער שנאיו:
>
> *"Our sister, may you be the mother of thousands of ten thousands; may your seed inherit the gate of those which hate them."*[5]

This is the blessing which Lavan[6] gave his sister Rivkah when she left to marry Yitzchak.

Why, at such special moments do we use the blessings of the malevolent Lavan, alias Bilam?

This question is even more baffling in the light of the following teaching of Chazal:

> *"Our sister, may you be the mother of thousands of ten thousands" – Why did Rivkah not have children until Yitzchak prayed for her? In order that the nations of the world should not say "Our prayer achieves results."*[7]

There was a danger that Lavan would receive the credit for Rivkah's having children, and so Rivkah was childless.

How long did this last?

> *Yitzchak was forty years old when he married Rivkah.*[8]
>
> *Yitzchak was sixty years old when [Rivkah] gave birth to them [Esav and Yaakov].*[9]

Rivkah did not give birth for twenty years, because people would attribute it to Lavan!

---

5. Bereishis 24:60.
6. Together with his mother.
7. *Yalkut Shimoni, Bereishis* ch.24 *remez* 109; *Bereishis Rabbah* 60:13.
8. Bereishis 25:20.
9. Ibid., v. 26.

She only has one pregnancy in her life, and one of the two children born is Esav. All this is the result of Lavan's blessing. So why do we bless a bride in such way?

9.2 "OUR SISTER"

One answer is based on a teaching concerning how to find the right wife:

> *Rava taught, "One who marries a woman should examine her brothers... We have learned that most sons resemble the mother's brothers."* [10]

The most dangerous phrase in Lavan's "blessing" was at the start: "our sister." He wanted Rivkah to give birth to "thousands of ten thousands" and they should all be like him. Terrifying!

We use the very same words, but with a totally different effect. We are saying that you should have "thousands of ten thousands" and they should all be like *us*! You are *our* sister.

Everything depends on who is speaking.

9.3 HOW TO KEEP AWAY THE FORCES OF EVIL

Another answer is based on an idea of R. Boruch Shimon Schneerson, who was the eminent Rosh Yeshivah of Tschebin. He is answering the question why we mention the blessing of the evil Bilam every morning when we enter shuls and he bases himself on a Midrash which teaches:

> *R' Acha son of Chanina taught: "It would have been fitting that the rebukes and threats of punishment should have been delivered by Bilam and the blessings of Bilam should have been delivered by Moshe.*

---

10. *Bava Basra* 110a.

However, if Bilam would have rebuked them, the Jews would have said, 'One who hates us is rebuking us.'[11]
If Moshe would have blessed them, the nations of the world would have said, 'One who loves them is blessing them.'[12]
Therefore the Holy One, Blessed is He, said, 'Let Moshe, who loves them, rebuke them; and let Bilam, who hates them, bless them.'"[13]

Since Bilam is the one who is delivering the blessings, so to speak,

The evil angel is forced to answer "Amen."[14]

There are evil forces in the world that try to prevent us from achieving our spiritual goals. Sometimes they can be deflected if they feel they are receiving their due. For example, these forces try to block the advent of Moshiach. Therefore, we find that the lineage of Moshiach is often not overtly respectable. Yaakov was married to two sisters; Yehudah and Tamar; David and Bas-Sheva, etc. For this reason, the evil forces have not prevented the births that lead towards Moshiach. They say "Amen."

We find the same idea in the area of prayer. There are evil spiritual forces which attempt to prevent our prayers from reaching heaven.

---

11. The Jews would think, "It is only because Bilam hates us that he is rebuking and cursing us, and he was not commanded by the Almighty to do so." Therefore they would not believe the threats.
12. The nations of the world would think, "It is only because Moshe loves them that he is blessing them, and he was not commanded to do so by the Almighty."
13. *Devarim Rabbah* 1:4
14. *Shabbos* 119b. The phrase is brought in the context of honoring the Sabbath: Rabbi Yosi son of Yehudah taught: "Two ministering angels accompany a man from the Synagogue to his home on the eve of the Sabbath. One is good and the other evil.
When he arrives home, and finds a lamp lit, the table laid, and his bed made, the good angel says, 'May it be His will that it should be like this next Sabbath,' and the evil angel is forced to answer 'Amen.'"

That is one reason given for saying the Amidah prayer quietly – so that it can reach its destination undetected.[15]

Similarly, we say chapters of Tehillim, called *Pesukei Dezimrah*. This phrase is usually translated as "verses of song." The Kabbalists, however, understand that it is related to the word זומר which means "pruning." These verses *prune away* the evil forces such that our prayers can proceed uninterrupted.[16]

This is also the reason we recite sections about the *ketores*, the incense, at the start of our morning prayers[17] and at the end.[18] The *ketores* has the power to ward off harmful forces, and even death.[19]

We can now understand why we say the blessing of the evil Bilam at the outset of the day's prayers. By reciting a verse of a wicked person, we appease the forces of evil, giving our prayers a better chance of not being impeded.

We asked why we use the blessing of a wicked person. The answer is *because* it is the blessing of a wicked person![20]

In a similar fashion, this idea explains why we bless brides with the words of the evil Lavan. We know that there are evil spiritual forces which try to prevent a bride and groom from establishing a

---

15. The repetition, however, is read out loud. This is not just to enable the congregation to hear it. The Arizal taught that, whereas the silent Amidah is a group of individuals praying together, the repetition is a single, unified prayer of the congregation and, as such, is much more powerful. Therefore, the forces of evil have no power to block it. (*Sefer Eitz Chayim, Sha'ar Ha'Amidah*, ch. 2.)
16. *Megaleh Amukos, parshas Beshalach*; *Shnei Luchos Habris, parshas Beshalach, Torah Ohr* 1 and 4; ibid., *parshas Ki Seitzei, Torah Ohr* 6.
17. We read Exodus 30:34-36, 7-8, and extracts from *Kerisos* 6a and Yerushalmi *Yoma* 4:5.
18. Again, we read an extract from *Kerisos* 6a. *Nusach Ashkenaz* omits this recitation of *ketores*. See Rema, *O.H.* 132:2 and *Mishnah Berurah* 17, ad loc.
19. See Bamidbar 17:9-15; *Shabbos* 89a; *Zohar*, Section 3, *parshas Pinchas*, p. 224a.
20. *HaBe'er* Torah journal, year 3 issue 2, "Topics connected to Prayer," R. Boruch Shimon Schneerson.

Torah home. This is the reason that the bride and groom customarily do not go outside alone without a *shomer*, someone to be with them for protection, from the day of the wedding until the end of the week of *sheva berachos*.

We use the blessing of Lavan in order that the evil angel is forced to answer "Amen."

Once again, we see the Almighty using Lavan, and his attempt to destroy our continuity, to defeat Lavan himself![21]

In order to deeply understand why cursing is so central to Lavan and Bilam, we need to examine the Torah's perspective on parent-child relationships.

---

21. See sections 7.12 and 7.13.

10

Honor, fear and cursing

10.1 WHY HAVE CHILDREN?

Children are expensive to raise. They often cause their parents much heartache. Why do so many people want to have children?

R. Dessler, in his famous *Kuntres Hachessed*, explains:

> *Everyone wants children. There are two motivations:*
> *1. We feel that children will be a continuation of ourselves after we leave the world.*
> *2. We have an innate need to have someone on whom to lavish love and kindness.*
> *That is why childless couples will often adopt children and raise them as their own. Some will even have a dog or other pet and lavish affection on them as if they were children. This is a clear indication of the deep-seated power of giving in the human soul.*[1]

We will see how the Torah relates to these two motivations.

---

1. *Michtav Me'Eliyahu*, vol. 1 p.36.

10.2 THE ALMOST IMPOSSIBLE COMMANDMENT

We know that we are meant to be happy about keeping the commandments of the Torah and not to seek opportunities to exempt ourselves from their observance. Therefore, it is quite surprising to read a statement in the Talmud about honoring parents:

> *Rabbi Yochanan said, "Happy is the one who never saw them!" When Rabbi Yochanan's mother was pregnant with him his father died. When she gave birth to him, she died.*[2]

Rabbi Yochanan came into the world as a baby without parents. Yet he considers himself very fortunate. Why?

Rashi explains:

> *"Happy is the one who never saw them!" - Because it is impossible to fulfil the honor due them to the level required, and one will be punished because of [lack of honor for] them.*

Rabbi Yochanan is happy not to have the obligation to honor parents because it is so hard to satisfy. What is so hard about it?

10.3 FOUR COMMANDMENTS

In fact, there is not only one positive commandment governing how we relate to parents, but two.

The first is in the Ten Commandments:[3]

> *Honor your father and your mother in order that your days may be long in the land which Hashem your G-d gives you.*[4]

---

2. *Kiddushin* 31b.
3. This is actually a misnomer, since there are actually fourteen commandments in this section of the Torah. The actual phrase is עשרת הדברים, which means "the ten statements." See Shemos 34:28, Devarim 4:13 and 10:4.

The second is in *parshas Kedoshim*:

> *Every man, his mother and his father shall you fear and keep My Sabbaths; I am Hashem your G-d.*[5]

There are several questions which require attention:

1. What is "honor" and what is "fear" – and what is the difference between them?

2. Why is long life the reward for honoring parents?

3. Why is this reward of long life given in "the land which Hashem your G-d gives you," i.e., in the land of Israel?

4. Why, in the commandment to honor parents, is the father mentioned first, whereas in the commandment to fear parents the mother is mentioned first?

Rashi answers this question:

> *"His mother and his father shall you fear" – Here "mother" precedes "father" since it is revealed to Him [the Almighty] that a son fears his father more than his mother;*[6] *concerning "honor" the father precedes the mother since it is revealed to Him that the son honors the mother more than the father,*[7] *since she wins him over with pleasant words.*[8]

What does this mean?

In what way does a son respect his mother more than his father?

How does this follow from the fact that "she wins him over with pleasant words"?

---

4. Shemos 20:12. See also Devarim 5:16 where this commandment is written with certain additions.
5. Vayikra 19:3.
6. Therefore, the Torah places the mother first to emphasize that she must also be feared.
7. Therefore, the Torah places the father first to emphasize that he must also be honored.
8. *Kiddushin* 30b-31a.

5. The verse in *parshas Kedoshim* starts in the singular, איש אמו ואביו, literally, "A man his mother and his father." This is in the singular form. However, the verse continues, תיראו, "You shall fear," in the plural form. What is the reason for the inconsistency?

Rashi explains that the verse means that all of you, plural, should each fear "his mother and his father." Is there any other approach as to why, specifically with regard to our approach to our parents, this change from singular to plural is employed?

6. The Ten Commandments[9] are divided into two groups of five. The first five concern the relationship between man and G-d. The second five have to do with relationships between man and man.[10] Why is the commandment to honor parents included in the first set of five, seeing as it concerns a relationship between people?

In addition to the positive commandments to honor and fear parents, there are two negative commandments concerning how we treat parents:

> *One who hits his father or his mother shall surely be put to death.*
> *One who steals a man and sells him, if he is found in his hand,*[11] *he shall surely be put to death.*
> *One who curses his father or his mother shall surely be put to death.*[12]

---

9. See footnote 3.
10. See Abarbanel, Shemos 20:2, question 5. Also see *Kli Yakar*, Shemos 20:12, who comments on this division and makes the observation that the first five all contain the name of G-d, whereas there is no such mention in any of the second five.
11. If he has sold the person whom he kidnapped, how is the victim "found in his hand"? Rashi explains that the phrase "found in his hand" means that witnesses saw that he kidnapped and sold the victim, i.e., the victim was "found in his hand" before the sale.
12. Shemos 21:15-17.

7. What is the significance of these two commandments?

8. Why does the prohibition to kidnap (anyone, not specifically a parent) interrupt the two parent-connected commandments, not to hit and not to curse parents?

10.4 THANK YOU FOR EVERYTHING

Let us examine *why* we need to honor parents. The *Sefer Hachinuch* explains:

> *It is fitting that a person acknowledges and acts kindly to one who has done good for him and not be unmindful and unappreciative, since this is an attribute which is repulsive, both in the eyes of G-d and man.*
> *One should bear in mind that one's father and mother are the reason that one exists in the world. Therefore it is only fitting that one should show them every possible respect and do them every service he can, since they brought him into the world and laboured greatly on his behalf during his childhood.*
> *Once a person has acquired this trait, he will ascend from it to be grateful for the good done for him by G-d, Who is the cause of his being and the cause of all his ancestors, reaching back to Adam.*[13]

According to the *Sefer Hachinuch*, the reason to honor parents is to develop and demonstrate the attribute of gratitude. This will bring us to have appreciation for what the Almighty does for us. This explains why honoring parents is in the first set of five – it is a key method for us to learn to develop a relationship with G-d.

We can also understand why it is such a difficult commandment to observe. The Hebrew word for "thanks" is הודאה. This word also

---

13. *Mitzvah* 33.

means "admission."[14] Why do we not have two different words for these two concepts, as in other languages?

The answer is that "thanks" is by definition an admission, i.e., an admission of debt – you have done something for me and I am in your debt. This explains why, paradoxically, it is easier to thank someone for a small favor done than for a lifetime of help. Honoring parents and acknowledging the enormity of the debt we owe them is almost impossible.

This is not the only reason we are commanded to honor our parents.

10.5 ANOTHER LINK IN THE CHAIN

We have already seen the approach of R. Samson Raphael Hirsch.[15] We quote it here more fully:

> *Our Tradition depends on the faithful transmission by parents to children, and on the willing acceptance by children from the hands of their parents. Therefore the continuance of G-d's whole great institution of Judaism is totally dependent on the theoretical and practical obedience of children to parents.*
> *It follows that honoring father and mother is the fundamental prerequisite for the eternity of the Jewish nation... without this bond, the chain of generations is broken, the Jewish past is lost for the future, and the Jewish nation ceases to exist.*[16]

We have to treat parents with respect if there is to be any Jewish continuity.

This understanding also explains why honoring parents is one of the first set of five. Without כבד את אביך there would be no אנכי – if there is no respect for parents there will be no belief in G-d!

---

14. See *Mishnah Shavuos* 6:1.
15. Section 6.2.
16. Commentary on Shemos 20:12.

Furthermore, we have another insight as to why it is so hard to honor parents. Children do not want to simply follow what their parents do. There is an urge to "go out and do my own thing." Total submission to the belief system and lifestyle of parents is very challenging.

It is illuminating to see what R. Hirsch writes about "inheritance." He bases himself on the following teaching of the Talmud:

> *Non-Jews are not subject to inheritance* (נחלה).[17]

They do inherit their parents, but do not have the laws of inheritance of Jews, for example that the first born receives a double portion.

There are two words in Hebrew for inheritance: נחלה and ירושה. Non-Jews have ירושה but not נחלה. The word ירושה, from the root ירש, is related to the idea of "driving out."[18] The younger, stronger generation pushes away the older. Non-Jews do have this type of inheritance.

The Jewish idea of inheritance is נחלה, from the word נחל, meaning "river." The idea being conveyed is that the next generation continues the flow of its parents.[19] Non-Jews do not have this.

10.6 HONOR AND FEAR

We now need to examine the difference between "honor" and "fear." We learn in the Talmud:

> *Our Rabbis taught: What is "fear" and what is "honor"?*
> *"Fear" means one does not stand in his [the father's] place, one does not sit in his place, one does not contradict him, and one does not even decide like him in an argument.*[20]

---

17. *Yevamos* 62a.
18. See, for example, Devarim 2:24,31.
19. R. Hirsch on Bereishis 9:22.

> *"Honor" means one feeds, gives to drink, clothes, covers, takes in and takes out.*[21]

At first sight, the distinction seems to be that "fear" means refraining from doing things we are not supposed to do and "honor" refers to the positive things we need to do. This is true, but there is more.

If we examine the requirements of "honor," we find that they are all things which our parents did for us when we were children. They fed us and gave us to drink. They clothed us and covered us with a blanket at night. Before we could walk, they took us in and out.

In other words, we are repaying the debt which we owe them, i.e., showing gratitude.

What about "fear"?

The laws of fear also apply to a *rebbi,* one's teacher of Torah. The Shulchan Aruch, in the section dealing with how to treat one's *rebbi*, says:

> *One should not sit in his place, nor decide like him in an argument in his presence, nor contradict him.*[22]

The laws of "fear" are to instill the obedience and deference such that one will listen to and be prepared to receive the Torah which is being taught.[23]

---

20. If a father is having a disagreement with someone, the son is not even allowed to say, "My father is right." See *Shulchan Aruch* 240:2; *Tur Y.D.* 240, quoting Remah, and second explanation of the *Beis Yosef*, ad loc., of Rashi on *Kiddushin* 31b, s.v. *velo machrio.* (Cf. the first explanation of the *Beis Yosef.*) The reason is that the son is regarding himself as an authority to decide whether his father is right or wrong, and this is totally inappropriate.
21. *Kiddushin* 31b.
22. *Y.D.* 242:16.
23. The *Shulchan Aruch* (*Y.D.* 242:19, quoting *Kesubos* 96a) states: "All the tasks which a slave performs for his master, a student should perform for his teacher." This includes preparing food and drink. Why should a student perform these activities for his teacher – the teacher never needed to

We now see that the laws of "honor" correspond to "gratitude," the rationale of the *Sefer Hachinuch*, whereas the laws of "fear" correspond to the obedience required to receive the tradition transmitted by our parents and teachers, as explained by R. Hirsch.

It is now clear why the father is mentioned first in the context of "honor," whereas the mother is mentioned first in the context of "fear."

Who is the parent that is primarily concerned with feeding, giving drink and clothing the child? The mother. She takes care of and showers love on her children, speaking words of love, affection and encouragement. Therefore, the stronger feelings of gratitude are to the mother. There would be a stronger tendency to show her "honor." As such, the Torah mentions the father first to indicate that they must be honored equally.

However, in the context of "fear," the child has a stronger tendency to fear his father. The father is the one who has the responsibility to teach his children. They must be receptive to his words and obey him. Therefore, the Torah mentions the mother first to show that they must be "feared" equally.

It is remarkable to look back to what we saw at the start of the chapter concerning the reasons people want to have children. We quoted R. Dessler:

> *Everyone wants children. There are two motivations:*

---

perform them for the student!? The answer is that, unlike the relationship between a child and parent, where the reason for performing these tasks is gratitude, in the case of a student the reason is because they are "the tasks which a slave performs for his master," and their performance demonstrates the complete subservience of the student to his teacher. Therefore, the tasks are not listed individually as they are with regard to honoring parents, since each task is not important in its own right as an act of gratitude, but what is required is merely the overall idea of subservience.

1. We feel that children will be a continuation of ourselves after we leave the world.
2. We have an innate need to have someone on whom to lavish love and kindness.

The Torah acknowledges both of these deep and powerful desires. In response to the first, children are to develop "fear," a reverence which allows the parents to transmit their values and goals to the next generation.

Regarding the second, the Torah obliges gratitude and acknowledgment of the kindness performed by parents to their children. It is much easier and more fulfilling to give when our efforts are acknowledged and appreciated.

The needs and desires of fathers and mothers are fully satisfied.

We have seen:

- There are two positive commandments concerning our relationship with our parents – "honor" and "fear."
- "Honor" represents gratitude to parents.
- "Fear" is to guarantee the obedience required to ensure that children will follow the parents' directives and beliefs.
- The mother deserves more gratitude and, thereby, more honor. However, the father is mentioned first, in the command to honor parents, to indicate that he should be equally honoured.
- The father is the primary source of the child's tradition and, thereby, is more deserving of fear. However, the mother is mentioned first, in the command to fear, to indicate that she should be equally feared.
- These two ideas, gratitude and continuity of parents' tradition, acknowledge the two motivations for having children – the desire to "continue" after leaving the world and the need to "give."

10.7 HOW TO LIVE A LONG LIFE

Why is the reward for honoring parents a long life?

We have seen that there are two rationales underpinning our obligations towards our parents – gratitude and continuity of the tradition. The reward of long life is appropriate in the light of both of them.

Firstly, in the context of gratitude, the *Yalkut Me'am Loez* explains:

> *It is normal that when a person is old, he becomes a burden on his family members. They have to work hard for him and all the time he is asking for something else, just like a baby.*
> *Therefore the Torah tells us: "Do not view the efforts of caring for parents as burdensome, and ask yourself, 'When will I be rid of them?'"*
> *You should know that if you live to an old age, your children will similarly be distressed by you and will be looking forward to your death so that they can be rid of you, since that was your attitude towards your parents. The world runs according to "measure for measure" and the way you treat your parents will determine the way your children will treat you.*[24]

We treat our parents with "respect" and take care of them since that is what they did for us when we were children. Additionally, we will benefit from this later in life when our children will care for us as we did for our parents.

With this in mind we have an answer as to why the verse in *parshas Kedoshim* starts in the singular, איש אמו ואביו, "A man his mother and his father," and continues in the plural, תיראו, "You shall fear."

The *Ohr Hachayim* explains that if the father fears his parents, then the child will follow. Therefore, the verse starts in the singular, with

24. *Yalkut Me'am Loez* on Shemos 20:12.

one person, and continues in the plural, with the children following their parent's example.

In the context of the continuity of our tradition and of the Jewish people, as explained by R. Hirsch, we once again see that the reward is "measure for measure." Since we are ensuring the continued existence of the nation we ourselves receive a continued existence, i.e., long life.

Why, though, is the long life specifically in the land of Israel, "the land which Hashem your G-d gives you"?[25]

10.8 THE LAND OF CANAAN

Throughout the Torah, the land of Israel is referred to as "the land of Canaan." Who was Canaan?

> *The sons of Noah who came out of the ark were Shem, Cham, and Yefes, Cham being the father of Canaan.*[26]

Canaan was a grandson of Noah. The land of Israel was meant to belong to him. However, he lost it. Why?

After Noah leaves the ark, we read:

> *Noah began to be a man of the soil, and he planted a vineyard. He drank of the wine and became drunk, and uncovered himself in his tent. Cham, the father of Canaan, saw the nakedness of his father and told his two brothers outside. Shem and Yefes took the garment and placed it on both their shoulders. They walked backwards and covered their father's nakedness. Their faces were turned away and they did not see their father's nakedness.*
>
> *Noah awoke from his wine and realized what his lowliest son*

25. Shemos 20:12, Devarim 5:16.
26. Bereishis 9:18.

had done to him. He said, "Cursed is Canaan, a slave of slaves he shall be to his brothers."[27]

Why is Canaan cursed? Rashi tells us:

"Cham, the father of Canaan, saw" – Some Rabbis explain that Canaan saw [the nakedness of his grandfather] and told his father. That is why Canaan is mentioned in this context and cursed.

The indication that Canaan was the one to see and publicize his grandfather's shame is the phrase "Cham, the father of Canaan, saw."

We already know that Cham was the father of Canaan, so why write it again here? Furthermore, why is it relevant here what children Cham had?

The answer is that Canaan is the first to see Noah's nakedness and he reveals it to Cham. His grandfather's shame should have been kept as secret as possible. Cham, himself, shows no respect for his father, broadcasting the news of Noah's disgrace to his brothers.[28]

It is this lack of any respect to a father and grandfather that leads to Canaan, son of Cham, being cursed and, thereby, losing the land of Israel.

Canaan lost the land of Israel due to disrespect of parents. So nothing could be more appropriate as a reward for respecting parents than long life in the land of Canaan.

10.9 CURSING AND HITTING

We have seen[29] that there are two negative commandments concerning how we treat parents:

---

27. Ibid., vv. 20-25.
28. See Rashi on verse 22, who brings two views how Cham did much worse than merely publicize the nakedness of Noah.
29. Section 10.3.

> *One who* ***hits*** *his father or his mother shall surely be put to death.*
> *One who steals a man and sells him, if he is found in his hand, he shall surely be put to death.*
> *One who* ***curses*** *his father or his mother shall surely be put to death.*[30]

As we have learned, the two positive commandments of "honor" and "fear" are predicated on the ideas of gratitude and ensuring continuity. These two ideas are so fundamental that they are also formulated in the negative manner.

Hitting someone is the strongest expression that one has no "fear" for that person. One goes right up to him and strikes him. Cursing, though, can be done from a distance or even without the knowledge of the person being cursed, and does not demonstrate a lack of fear.

If hitting is the opposite of "fear," then it should follow that cursing is the opposite of "honor" and showing gratitude for what parents have done for us.

How is this so?

The Hebrew word for "honor" is כבוד. The root of this word is כבד, which is usually translated as "heavy." This has a negative connotation, and a more accurate translation would be "weighty," i.e., having substance, significance and importance.[31] When we treat someone with "honor," we are expressing that the person is important to us.

The Hebrew word meaning "to curse" is קלל. The root of the word is קל, which means "light," insignificant, without substance.[32]

When a person curses his parent he is proclaiming "You do not have any significance to me at all!" That is the opposite of "honor."[33]

---

30. Shemos 21:15-17.
31. See R. Hirsch on Shemos 20:12.
32. See Rashi on Devarim 21:23 and R. Hirsch on Shemos 22:27.

Why, though, does kidnapping interrupt the thematically connected prohibitions of hitting and cursing parents?

10.10 THE KIDNAPPED CHILD

How is it possible that a child could come to hit or curse a parent?

Cursing is the opposite of gratitude. A child could come to curse a parent if the child had never benefitted from the parent, had never been given food, drink or clothing. How could this occur? If the child was kidnapped, he would not receive benefit from his parents.

Hitting is the opposite of the "fear" and obedience required to continue our tradition. A child could curse a parent if he was never taught about his tradition by his parents. That, too, could occur if the child was kidnapped. In fact, we call someone who was never taught Torah a תינוק שנשבה, "a captive child."[34]

The common denominator between hitting and cursing a parent is that the child has been kidnapped. That is why kidnapping is placed between the two prohibitions.

---

33. We saw in section 10.6 that, in the context of "honor," the father is mentioned first, since there would be a stronger tendency to show gratitude to the mother; in the context of "fear," it is the mother who is mentioned first, since there is a greater tendency to fear the father. Since "hitting" corresponds to "fear," why is the mother not mentioned first in the prohibition to hit father or mother?
When there is a question whether to show respect to either one's father or mother, if they are married to each other the law is that the father has precedence. (*Shulchan Aruch*, *Y.D.* 240:14) As such, the default is to always write the father first. The Torah reverses the order *once* to convey the idea that in spite of the stronger tendency to show "fear" to the father, the mother should be equally feared. There is no need to reverse the order again. Furthermore, since the prohibitions of hitting and cursing parents are in such close proximity, the requirements of consistency of style might have some significance.
34. See *Shabbos* 68a.

It should be mentioned that children can be in a state of being kidnapped even while they are living in the same house as their parents, being deprived of their physical and emotional needs. So too, they can remain ignorant of their heritage because their parents never taught them. Today, it is often the teacher who has to provide both the knowledge of heritage as well as provide for the emotional, if not the physical, needs of the student.

10.11 WHY DO THEY CURSE?

We now understand why "cursing" is central to Lavan and Bilam.[35] They have no gratitude whatsoever. The expression of this is "cursing" because no one else is important to them. There is no כבוד, only קללה!

It is fascinating to examine the portion of Torah which exemplifies the opposite of ingratitude – the bringing of *bikkurim*, first fruits, to the Temple.

After the toil required to grow fruits and crops, when the first produce finally appears, it may not be eaten, but is taken to the Temple and given to the priest. This is an act of appreciation demonstrating an acknowledgement that everything is really from Hashem. The bringing of *bikkurim* is accompanied by a declaration:

> *You shall come to whoever will be the Priest in those days, and you shall say: "I declare today to Hashem your G-d that I have come to the land which Hashem swore to our fathers to give us."*[36]

Rashi comments:

> *"And you shall say" – That you are not ungrateful.*

---

35. See also section 17.5.
36. Devarim 26:3.

This commandment focuses on appreciation. Even though it is obvious that the event is occurring in the land of Israel, we mention that we are in the land of Israel in order to show our gratitude. Not only do we appreciate the fruit, but even the land.

When the priest takes the basket of first fruits, the one who brought the *bikkurim* makes a further declaration, which starts with the words:

"An Aramean [sought to] destroy my forefather."[37]

Who is the "Aramean"? Rashi explains:

Lavan wanted to uproot everything when he pursued Yaakov.[38]

Precisely at the moment when we are focusing on gratitude, we remember one of the most ungrateful men in our history. Lavan only had sons in the merit of Yaakov[39] – and yet wanted to kill him. See what ingratitude can cause!

10.12 HARMFUL WORDS

It is horrifying to see the harm Lavan causes through cursing. After Yaakov and family flee from Lavan's home, Lavan pursues them and, when he catches up with them, he accuses Yaakov of theft:

"Why did you steal my gods?"[40]

As we saw in chapter 7,[41] Lavan's daughter Rachel had taken them, in an attempt to disconnect her father from idolatry.

Yaakov, unaware that Rachel had stolen them, declares:

---

37. Ibid., v. 5. This translation follows *Targum*, *Sifrei*, and Rashi; cf. Rashbam, Seforno.
38. See section 7.10.
39. See section 7.2.
40. Bereishis 31:30.
41. Section 7.12.

"With whomever you find your gods, he shall not live!" [42]

Rashi, chillingly, comments:

> *"Shall not live" – From that curse Rachel died on the journey [back to Israel].*

Even though Rachel's intent was to disconnect her father from idol worship, she is punished for the pain her act of theft caused her father. The punishment, aptly, comes by means of a curse, a reminder of her lack of gratitude to her father.

It is very ironic that Lavan's allegation of theft leads to the death of his own daughter!

In a similar vein, we saw[43] the harmful impact of Lavan's blessing of his sister Rivkah – twenty years pass until she becomes capable of having a child, she is only ever pregnant once, and one of the children born is Esav.

10.13 THE AFFLICTION

Another statement Lavan makes also seems to have a detrimental impact on Yaakov's family.

In the covenant that Lavan makes with Yaakov, he says:

> *"If you will afflict my daughters and if you will take wives besides my daughters, there may be no man between us, but see, G-d is a witness between me and you."*[44]

What does he mean by the word "afflict"?

It is interesting to note the next occurrence of the word.

The daughter of Yaakov, granddaughter of Lavan, goes out to see the women of the surrounding area:

---

42. Bereishis 31:32.
43. Section 9.1.
44. Bereishis 31:50.

> *Shechem, son of Chamor the Chivite, the prince of the land saw her, and he took her and he lay with her and he afflicted her."*[45]

The word seems to be used differently here! Here it seems to mean forced relations. However, with regard to Lavan's condition in the covenant he makes with Yaakov, it does not seem to mean that.

We can infer this because, concerning Yom Kippur, we are commanded:

> *You shall afflict yourselves.*[46]

Besides the affliction of not eating or drinking, one of the prohibited activities on Yom Kippur is marital relations. The Talmud[47] asks how we know that abstinence in this area is included in the precept to "afflict" ourselves.

The answer given is that it is learned from the verse which Lavan said to Yaakov, "If you will *afflict* my daughters," which is understood to mean *deprivation* of conjugal rights.

The Talmud attempts to refute this proof by adducing the verse of Shechem's rape of Dinah, "and he lay with her and he *afflicted* her," to show that "affliction" is the very opposite of abstinence in this area.

The answer given is that the "affliction" inflicted by Shechem refers to the deprivation of subsequent relations after the initial rape.[48]

The connection between the verse in which Lavan feigns concern that there should be no "affliction" of his daughters and the "affliction" of Dinah is not happenstance.[49] Once again, Lavan's words

---

45. Ibid., 34:2.
46. Vayikra 16:31, 23:27, 32; Bamidbar 29:7.
47. *Yoma* 77a-b.
48. At this point Dinah *did* desire to be with Shechem.
49. When the brothers hear of the indignity perpetrated to their sister, we read: "They seethed with anger, for [Shechem] had committed an outrage in Israel." (Bereishis 34:7) The word for "outrage" is נבלה, which is from the

have dire consequences.[50] The result is a relationship which is the antithesis of holiness and family, and in which the ability to produce children is denied.

10.14 HOW MANY CURSE WORDS DO YOU KNOW?

To fully appreciate the association between Lavan, Bilam and cursing, we need to look further at the Hebrew word for "curse."

When the Almighty commands Avraham to leave his homeland, He tells him:

ואברכה מברכיך ומקללך אאר...[51]

---

root נבל. This word has the letters of the name לבן and furthermore, נבל, as we will see in chapter 17, is a continuation of the life and essence of לבן.

50. It is fascinating to note that *Pirkei D'Rebbe Eliezer* (ch. 38) teaches that, from the rape of Dinah by Shechem, a daughter was born. Dinah's brothers wanted to kill the baby, claiming that it would bring shame on the family. Yaakov took a metal band, wrote a holy name on it, and hung it around the baby's neck. The angel Michael took the baby to Egypt, to the home of Potiphera, whose wife was childless. This woman raised the baby as a daughter and she was the Osnat who became Yosef's wife. Osnat, a girl separated from her family, marries Yosef, a man separated from his family, and yet they stay true to their tradition, so much so that we bless our sons each week with the blessing that they should be like Ephraim and Menashe, the sons of Yosef and Osnat.
The word used for the "metal band" on which Yaakov wrote the holy name is ציץ, *"tzitz,"* a word generally used in connection with the golden band worn on the forehead of the High-priest. As we saw, in section 4.4, the *tzitz* represents continuous connection of mind – "it shall be worn on Aharon's forehead... it shall be on his forehead *continuously*" (Shemos 26:36-38). The High-priest had to touch it again and again to constantly remind himself that he was wearing it. (We learn the obligation to be constantly aware of the *tefillin* we wear from the *tzitz*. See *Shabbos* 12a, *Yoma* 7a, *Menachos* 36b.)
Osnat will be totally separated from her family, in a foreign country and surrounded by an alien culture. The *tzitz*, with the inscription of a holy name, will ensure her continued connection to her tradition.
51. Bereishis 12:3.

What is the translation of these words? Most English renditions say something like:

> *"I will bless those who bless you and one who curses you I will curse..."*

The difficulty is that two different roots are used in the phrase "and one who curses you I will curse." One is קלל and the other ארר. What is the difference in meaning between these two words?

There is no such thing as a perfect synonym in the Torah. The shades of meaning that differentiate between the similar words must be understood.

The Malbim's commentary contains many beautiful examples of subtle distinctions between apparent synonyms. Concerning the words קלל and ארר his commentary[52] is illuminating. He explains that the word קלל relates to the articulation of the curse, without any connection to its impact. ארר indicates the effect of the curse on the one being cursed.[53] When the Torah refers to a curse issuing from the Almighty, the word ארור is used, since the curse will always have an impact, no one having the power to prevent it.[54] Conversely, when referring to man cursing Hashem, the root ארר is never used, since our curses cannot harm the Almighty.[55]

With this distinction, let us return to the verse in question:

52. Bamidbar 22:6.
53. For example, in Devarim 28:20, we read "Hashem will send in your midst המארה." Rashi explains that the word המארה, which is from the root ארר, means חסרון, i.e., lack or attrition.
54. The Malbim mentions an exception - Bereishis 8:21. There, after the flood, Hashem promises: לא אסף לקלל עוד את האדמה בעבור האדם – "I will not curse the land again because of man." Perhaps the explanation is that Hashem is saying that He will not even verbalize the words of a curse, let alone actually cause damage by means of a curse. The examples of the use of ארור are where the Almighty is actually cursing, not where He says He will not.
55. For example, see Vayikra 24:15.

ואברכה מברכיך ומקללך אאר...[56]

We now appreciate the full significance of the promise. Someone who merely *verbalizes* a curse towards Avraham, even without it having any adverse impact, will be punished with a curse which will really cause harm.

We have learned that the word קלל (to curse) is connected to the word קל, implying a lack of respect. It is so appropriate that it is Bilam, a man with no respect for parents, who is the most famous man to ever attempt to curse us.

If, as we have seen, cursing is associated with a lack of connection between fathers and sons, then we might expect blessing to be linked to the relationship between fathers and sons.

The Hebrew word for "blessing" is ברכה.

Hebrew words are based on three-letter roots. The commentary of R. Samson Raphael Hirsch contains many examples of the idea that three-letter roots which start with the same *two* letters are thematically connected.

Words which start with בר are connected with the idea of breaking out of restriction or a bringing out from potential to actuality.[57] Examples include ברא, "He created" and ברח, "he fled." The root בר, itself, is the Aramaic word for "a son," as in the name ר' שמעון בר יוחאי, "Rebbe Shimon the son of Yochai."[58] So blessings are, by definition, linked to creating something new, such as having children!

It is remarkable to observe that the word ארר also is closely related to the idea of a lack of connection with children.

Letters which are phonetically similar are often interchangeable.[59]

56. Bereishis 12:3.
57. See R. Hirsch on Bereishis 1:1.
58. For three examples of the use of the word בר meaning "son" in Tenach see Ezra 5:1-2.
59. Rashi (Vayikra 19:17) lists some of the interchangeable letters.

R. Hirsch comments on the first occurrence of the root ארר, when the snake is cursed,[60] that the word is connected to ערירי, the letters *aleph* and *ayin* being very similar phonetically and, therefore, sometimes interchangeable. The word ערירי means childless![61]

To appreciate the full depth of the connection of cursing and Bilam, we need to return once more to the promise made by Hashem to Avraham and examine it with a remarkable tool:

ואברכה מברכיך ומקללך אאר...[62]

One of the tools used in Torah-interpretation is *gematria*. Each Hebrew letter has a numerical value: א=1, ב=2, etc. This continues until י=10. Then כ=20, ל=30, etc. until ק=100. Finally, ר=200, ש=300 and ת=400.[63] The numerical totals obtained from summing the letter-values of words, phrases and sentences, can have deep significance.

One of the most famous examples of this tool in action is found in a comment of Rashi. When Yaakov sends messengers to his brother, Esav, the message he conveys starts with the words:

עם לבן גרתי – *"I dwelled with Lavan"* (Bereishis 32:4).

Rashi[64] observes that the *gematria*, of the word גרתי is 613 – the number of commandments in the Torah.[65] Yaakov is telling Esav, "Although I dwelled with the evil Lavan, I still kept all of the 613 commandments."

Similarly, if ideas have the same *gematria* they are often thematically linked.

---

60. Bereishis 3:14.
61. For example, see Bereishis 15:2.
62. Bereishis 12:3.
63. It should be noted that there are many systems of *gematria*. For example, some assign different values to the final letters. The system we have mentioned is the most famous and the most widely encountered.
64. See section 5.1.
65. *Makkos* 23b.

Our Rabbis point out that the *gematria* of the word יין, wine, is the same as that of סוד, secret, both having a numerical value of 70. Based on this they observe, "When *wine* enters [a person], a *secret* will come out."[66]

The *Ba'al Haturim*, who makes extensive use of *gematria* in his commentary, makes the following astonishing comments:

"ואברכה מברכיך" – בגימטריא "כהנים המברכים **בניך**"
"מקללך אאר" – בגימטריא "**בלעם** הבא לקלל **בניך**"

The *gematria* of ואברכה מברכיך, "I will bless those who bless you" is the same as that of כהנים המברכים **בניך**, "priests who bless *your sons*."[67]

The blessing is specifically connected with "your sons." It is the priests, exemplifying the holiness which Bilam tries to destroy, who are the ones to bless our sons.

Even more remarkable is the comment on the next phrase of the verse:

The *gematria* of מקללך אאר (422), *"and one who curses you I will curse,"* is the same as that of **בלעם** הבא לקלל **בניך**, *"**Bilam** who comes to curse your **sons**"*!

Amazing! Who is the one who curses? Bilam! Who does he come to curse? Your sons! He tries to destroy the connection between fathers and sons. It is so appropriate that these ideas are alluded to in the blessing given to Avraham, the *father* of our nation.[68]

We have seen:

- In addition to the two positive commandments regarding parents, there are two negative commandments.

---

66. *Eiruvin* 65a, *Sanhedrin* 38a.
67. See *Iturei Bikkurim* on the *Ba'al Haturim*, ad loc., who explains how the computation is made, such that the *gematrias* of these two phrases tally. Also see *Ohr Hatorah*, authored by R. Moshe Tzuriel (Bnei Brak, 5743), p. 16.
68. See sections 8.1 and 11.2

- The first is the prohibition against hitting parents. This corresponds to the positive command to fear them.
- The second is the prohibition against cursing them. This corresponds to the positive command to honor them as an expression of gratitude. This is indicated by the fact that the word for "honor," כבוד, is related to the word כבד, meaning "weighty," and the word for "curse," קלל is related to the word קל, meaning "lightweight."
- So it is not surprising to find that both Lavan and Bilam, who have no gratitude to parents, are the ones who curse us!

The opposite of Bilam is someone who honors his parents and is concerned to have a connection with them. We have learned[69] that someone like this will merit children who will honor him. Who was one of the most successful parents of all time, father to the greatest fathers and mothers, and how did he achieve it?

69. Section 10.7.

11

The father of fathers

11.1 THE FAMILY TREE

We have seen that where there is no connection to one's father, there is an inability to father sons.[1] Is the converse true? Does a respect for and connection with fathers confer the merit of producing sons, who in turn become fathers?

It is fascinating to examine who is the "father" of the Patriarchs and Matriarchs and to see why he merited this.

Let us study the family tree:

> *Terach was seventy years old when he fathered Avram, Nachor and Haran.*[2]

Who were the wives of Terach's sons?

> *Avram and Nachor married. The name of Avram's wife was Sarai. The name of Nachor's wife was Milkah, daughter of Haran, the father of Milkah and the father of Yiscah.*[3]

---

1. Section 7.2. We saw that, in his own merit, Lavan (לא–בן) is incapable of fathering sons.
2. Bereishis 11:26.
3. Ibid., v. 29.

Who was Yiscah (יסכה)? Rashi enlightens us:

> *"Yiscah" – She is Sarah.*[4]

Consider Terach's descendants:

Avraham is a son of Terach and Sarah (Yiscah) is his granddaughter.

Yitzchak is his grandson and Yaakov is his great-grandson respectively.

Rivkah is a daughter of Besuel, who is a son of Nachor and Milkah.[5] In other words, Rivkah is a great-granddaughter of Terach.

Rachel and Leah are daughters of Lavan,[6] who in turn is a son of Besuel.[7] So they are great-great-granddaughters of Terach.

Furthermore, four of Yaakov's children were born from Bilhah and Zilpah. Rashi tells us,

> *Bilhah and Zilpah were also daughters of Lavan, born from a concubine.*[8]

As such, they too are great-great-granddaughters of Terach.

So *all* our forefathers and mothers are direct descendants of Terach!

How did Terach, an idol worshipper and vendor of idols, merit fathering such offspring?

---

4. Rashi explains the connection between the name "Yiscah" and the identity of Sarah:
   She is referred to as "Yiscah" (יסכה) since she perceived (סוכה) with the holy spirit. Furthermore, the name יסכה is etymologically related to נסיכות, meaning "aristocratic" just as שרה is related to שררה, meaning "authority."
   Actually, at the time she was "Sara**i**." Only later is her name changed to "Sara**h**."
5. Bereishis 22:20, 23.
6. Ibid., 29:16.
7. Ibid., 28:5.
8. Rashi on Bereishis 31:50.

11.2 "THEY'RE NAMED AFTER YOU!"

The verses of the Torah tell us little about Terach. We are told he had three sons and that he journeyed with his family from Ur-Casdim to go to Canaan, arriving at Charan and staying there. He died at the age of two hundred and five, in Charan.[9] What was special about him?

Let us look at the names he gives his three sons:

ויחי תרח שבעים שנה ויולד את אברם את נחור ואת הרן:

Terach was seventy years old when he fathered Avram, Nachor and Haran.[10]

Each one of the sons is named with Terach's parents in mind.

Avram (אברם) is a contraction of the words אב רם, which mean "father is elevated."[11]

Haran (הרן) is connected to the word הורה,[12] and alludes to "our parents."

What about the name "Nachor"? If we look at the birth of Terach we find the answer:

---

9. Bereishis 11:31-32.
10. Ibid., v. 26.
11. Rashi (Bereishis 17:5) explains that the name אברם is a contraction of אב ארם (Av-Aram) – "father of Aram," the birthplace of Avraham. The Almighty subsequently changes this name to אברהם (Avraham) – a contraction of אב–המון (Av-hamon), meaning "the father of many [nations]." (See Rashi, ad loc., as to why the letter *reish* remains in the name.) Does this contradict the explanation we have written?

    An important tool in looking at names in the Torah is the fact that there may be more than one layer of meaning to a name. For example, the name בנימין (Binyamin) has more than one meaning. (See Rashi, on Bereishis 35:18, where two explanations of the name are given.)

    Similarly, the name אברם can have more than one meaning. Terach may have had in mind אב–רם, "father is elevated," whereas the Almighty had in mind אב–ארם, "father of Aram."
12. See, for example, Bereishis 49:26: "May your father's blessings add to the blessings of *my parents*" – הורי.

***Nachor** was twenty-nine years old when he fathered Terach.*[13]

Terach is the first man in the Torah to name a son after his father. His son, Nachor, is named after his father, Nachor!

Clearly, Terach had great respect for his father and therefore he merits children who will be the ultimate fathers and mothers.

It is relevant to quote the Midrash:

> *The Holy one, Blessed is He, said..."Who is the person who preceded with honoring his parents, and I did not reward him with children?"*[14]

If there is a bond with parents, then there will be children.[15]

11.3 COME IN PEACE

Not only does Terach merit fathering the Patriarchs and Matriarchs, but he even repents from his idolatrous ways. How do we know this?

When the Almighty makes a covenant with Avraham, He promises,

> *"You shall come to your fathers in peace and be buried at a good old age."*[16]

Rashi is bothered by a question:

> *"To your fathers" – His father is an idol worshipper and He is informing him that he will join him!? This teaches us that Terach repented.*

---

13. Bereishis 11:24.
14. *Midrash Tanchuma, Kedoshim* para. 15.
15. It is clear that there are people who do have great respect for and connection with parents and still do not merit having children. Innumerable factors influence the divine running of the world. One of the factors, though, is that respect for parents creates a strong merit for having children.
16. Bereishis 15:15.

The *Be'er Basadeh*, one of the super-commentaries on Rashi, asks,

> *How does Rashi know that Terach repented? Perhaps he has a portion in the World to Come in the merit of his son Avraham! We know that there is a Talmudic principle "A son can give merit to his father."*[17]

He offers a beautiful textual inference, which is based on an important principle in studying Torah texts:

If the order of words seems strange, the reason should be investigated.

The verse does *not* say:

> *"You shall come in peace to your fathers."*

This would imply that "your coming shall be in peace."
Instead it says:

> *"You shall come to your fathers in peace."*

Now the phrase "in peace" relates to the fathers.
The implication is that the fathers[18] were already in peace, having repented.
The Midrash gives an amazing inference to show that Terach has a portion in the world-to-come:

> *Rebbe Abba son of Cahana taught: "Anyone whose name is doubled exists in both worlds. 'Noach, Noach,'*[19] *'Avraham, Avraham,'*[20] *'Yaakov, Yaakov,'*[21] *'Moshe Moshe,'*[22] *'Shmuel,*

---

17. "ברא מזכי אבא" - *Sanhedrin* 104a.
18. If we are referring to Terach, why is the plural used, "to your *fathers*"? See the *Maskil Le'David* who answers that the other father is Adam, the first man. It is widely taught in kabbalistic writings that Avraham's life was a rectification of the sin of Adam. (See Arizal, *Sha'ar Hapesukim, Lech Lecha*.)
19. Bereishis 6:9.
20. Ibid., 22:11 and 25:19.
21. Ibid., 46:2.

Shmuel'[23] *'Peretz, Peretz.'"*[24]
They asked him: "Is it not also written, 'These are the generations of ***Terach: Terach*** *[fathered Avram, Nachor and Haran]'?"*[25]
He answered them: "Even he has a portion in two worlds. Our father Avraham was not gathered in [i.e., did not die] until he was informed that his father, Terach, had repented, as it says, 'You shall come to your fathers in peace.' Avraham said to the Holy One, Blessed is He, 'Master of the world, I stored up good deeds in this world, and I am going to my fathers?' The Holy One, Blessed is He, informed him, 'By your life, your father repented.' Therefore, his name is doubled."[26]

---

22. Shemos 3:4. The reason that we have not placed a comma between the two uses of "Moshe" is based on the *Zohar*, section 3, page 187b, which teaches that there is no interruption between the two names "Moshe Moshe," whereas there is an interruption in "Avraham, Avraham."
The idea conveyed here is that every doubling of a name has an "interruption" between the two names. The cases of Noach, Peretz and Terach and one of the instances of the doubling of Avraham, are not direct speech and the second use of the name starts a new clause. The cases of Yaakov, Moshe, Shmuel and the other instance of the doubling of Avraham, are all direct speech, with the Almighty addressing each of them with a doubling of their name. However, unlike the others who have a *"p'sik,"* a cantillation break between the two names, there is no such break in "Moshe Moshe."
The kabbalistic understanding is that the double use of the name indicates the dual existence, in the higher world and down here on earth. The essence here on earth is not the same as its spiritual source in the higher world. This is expressed with an interruption between the two names. Moshe, however, was on such a high level here on earth that his earthly being was just like his spiritual source on high. As such, there is no interruption between the two names.
23. I Shmuel 3:10.
24. Ruth 4:18.
25. Bereishis 11:27.
26. *Midrash Tanchuma, Shemos* para. 18.

We have seen in the *Sefer Hachinuch*[27] that respect for parents, with the gratitude involved, is the stepping-stone to developing a relationship with G-d.

Lavan despises his parents, never repents, and is incapable of having sons.

Terach is the antithesis of Lavan – he has great respect for his father (as evidenced by the naming of all of his sons after his father). Thus his ultimate achievement is not at all surprising – he eventually repents and he is the one who is the father of all the Patriarchs and Matriarchs.

27. See section 10.4.

12

Esav – rough and ruddy

12.1 ESAV IN NIMROD'S CLOTHING

Lavan is the epitome of disconnection from one's father.

Esav is the exact opposite.

When Rivkah sends Yaakov to receive the blessings from Yitzchak, she disguises him as Esav:

> *Rivkah took the special* (החמדות) *clothing of Esav, her older son, which were with her in the house, and she clothed Yaakov, her younger son.*[1]

What was special about the clothing? Rashi gives two explanations for the word החמדות. The first is that they were clean. The second explanation is:

> *He [Esav] had appropriated* (חמד) *them from Nimrod.*

These were royal garments. We know that Nimrod was a king.[2] When did Esav wear these special clothes?

---

1. Bereishis 27:15.
2. Section 8.1.

Rabban Shimon ben Gamliel said: "When I used to serve my father, I served him in dirty clothing, and when I used to go out I would wear nice clothing in order that I should appear at my best in the public domain.[3]
Esav, though, when he served his father, wore royal garments, as it says, "the special (החמדות) clothing of Esav, her older son."[4]
The word חמודות refers to royal clothing. Esav said, 'My father deserves that I should serve him in royal clothing.'"[5]

This teaching carries extra weight when we remember that Rabban Shimon ben Gamliel was the son of Rabban Gamliel, Nasi (prince) of the Jewish community in Israel.

He eventually succeeded his father as Nasi and was in turn succeeded by his son, Rebbe Yehudah Hanasi. We are talking about the "royal family." Even so, Rabban Shimon ben Gamliel did not wear "royal clothing" to serve his Nasi father.

Esav did better than this – he served his father in a remarkable manner. He wore החמודות, which he had appropriated (חמד) from Nimrod.

From where did these garments come? The Midrash teaches that before the building of the Mishkan (tabernacle), it was permissible to offer sacrifices on private altars. The holy service was then performed by firstborns.[6] Initially, the Holy One, Blessed is He, clothed Adam in special robes of a High Priest, since he was

3. It is appropriate to mention the fact that R. Shlomo Zalman Auerbach, *zt"l* used to straighten his clothing and made sure he looked his best before *entering* his home and greeting his wife.
4. Bereishis 27:15.
5. *Pesikta Rabbasi* 23.
6. The firstborns were the priests until they lost this status as a result of the sin of the golden calf, when the service was transferred to the descendants of Aharon.

humanity's firstborn.[7] This was the clothing which Esav wore to serve his father – robes of a High Priest, used for holy service!

There is a special aspect to this display of respect, in that Nimrod was the instigator of the tower of Bavel. We saw that the purpose of building the tower was to oppose fathers, the Almighty and Avraham.[8] Esav is using the clothing of Nimrod to honor his father!

12.2 TIME TO MARRY

At what age did Esav marry?

> *Esav was forty years old when he took as wives Yehudis, daughter of Be'eri the Hittite, and Bosmas, daughter of Elon the Hittite.*[9]

Rashi comments:

> *"Forty years old" – Esav is compared to a pig, as it says, "the wild pig out of the wood ravages it."*[10] *The pig, when it lies down, stretches out its cloven hoofs, as if to say, "See I am a pure animal!"*[11] *Similarly, there are those who rob and*

---

7. *Aggadas Bereishis*, ch. 43. The continuation of this *midrash* teaches that Adam gave the robes to his son, Shes. They were subsequently passed to Mesushelach, Noach, Shem, Avraham and then Yitzchak. Yitzchak then gave them to his firstborn son, Esav. This disagrees with the interpretation we quoted, from Rashi, that Esav "appropriated (חמד) them from Nimrod." Rashi, though, can agree with the idea that the robes were originally given by the Almighty to Adam for the purpose of holy service.
8. Sections 8.1-8.3.
9. Bereishis 26:34.
10. Tehillim 80:14. This verse alludes to Esav. See Rashi, ad loc.
11. There are two conditions for an animal to be kosher. Firstly, it chews the cud, and secondly, it has cloven hoofs. The pig is the only animal which has the external sign of kosher animals, i.e., it has cloven hoofs, and is still not kosher, lacking the internal sign of chewing the cud (Vayikra 11:7). The analogy is that Esav resembles the pig, externally pretending to be upstanding, while internally being evil.

appropriate, while pretending to be decent. For forty years, Esav preyed on other men's wives, raping them. When he was forty years old he said, "My father married at forty,[12] *I will do the same."*

Esav, even though he is evil, does try to emulate his father. If his father married at forty, Esav will attempt to do the same.

12.3 PREY WITH THE MOUTH

What did Yitzchak think of his son, Esav? After the birth of Esav and Yaakov, we are told:

The boys grew up. Esav became one who knows trapping, a man of the field. Yaakov was a plain man, dwelling in tents. Yitzchak loved Esav because prey was in his mouth, but Rivkah loved Yaakov.[13]

What is the meaning of "because prey was in his mouth"?

Furthermore, was Yitzchak unaware that Yaakov was the righteous son, not Esav?

Rashi comes to our aid, giving two explanations. The first teaches:

"In his mouth" – As the Targum translates, i.e., in the mouth of ***Yitzchak****.*

The Targum translates the phrase "because prey was in his mouth" as "because he ate from his prey." In other words, Yitzchak loved Esav because of the food which Esav fed him, the food which was in the *mouth of Yitzchak*.

This is not easy to understand. Is Yitzchak's love based on culinary considerations?

Rashi's second explanation is:

---

12. See Bereishis 25:20.
13. Bereishis 25:27-28.

The midrashic explanation is "in the mouth of ***Esav****"; he [Esav] trapped him [Yitzchak] and deceived him with his words.*

What was the deception? Rashi on the phrase *"who knows trapping"* explains:

"Who knows trapping" – To trap and deceive his father with his mouth. He would ask him, "Father, how does one tithe salt and straw?" His father thought that he was meticulous in his performance of commandments.

Yitzchak was aware that Yaakov was the Torah scholar. Explaining the phrase describing Yaakov, "dwelling in tents," Rashi informs us:

"Dwelling in tents" – The tent of Shem and the tent of Ever.

Shem and Ever were two of the outstanding sages of their time. We know that when Rivkah experienced difficulties during her pregnancy, she went to consult the house of study of Shem.[14] On the way to Lavan, Yaakov studies for fourteen years in the house of study of Ever.[15] If Yaakov is spending his time studying, whereas Esav is hunting in the field, the difference between them should be quite apparent.

So why did Yitzchak love Esav?

12.4 STRAW AND SALT

A tool in comprehension of Torah passages is the realization that many times, when Rashi writes two explanations, they are not arguing with each other, but are complementary.[16]

An example concerns the place where Sarah died:

Sarah died in Kiryas Arba, which is Hevron...[17]

---

14. Rashi on Bereishis 25:22.
15. Rashi on Bereishis 28:9. Shem was no longer alive at this point in time.
16. See *Klalim B'Rashi*, printed at the end of *Maseches Berachos* [Vilna].

The name "Kiryas Arba" literally means "City of Four." Who are the "four" after whom the city is named?

Rashi explains:

> *"Kiryas Arba" – After the four giants who lived there – Achiman, Sheshai, Talmoi*[18] *and their father. Another explanation is that it is after the four couples who were buried there, man and wife – Adam and Chava, Avraham and Sarah, Yitzchak and Rivkah, Yaakov and Leah.*

Although these two explanations seem to be mutually exclusive, the Maharal, in his commentary *Gur Arye*, teaches that this is not so. He writes that the fact that the land could raise such giants testifies to its *physical* quality. This physical quality indicates that it also had a parallel *spiritual* quality making it suitable as a burial site for these four remarkable couples.

So the two explanations are, in fact, complementary.

Similarly, the two explanations as to whether the "prey" was in the "mouth of Yitzchak" or "the mouth of Esav" are complementary.

Yitzchak loved Esav because he envisaged a state of affairs in which Yaakov would be the Torah scholar who would be supported by his brother, Esav. This is akin to the relationship that would occur in the future between two of Yaakov's sons, Yissochor and Zevulun.[19]

Rashi's first explanation teaches us that Esav, the hunter, was the one who provided Yitzchak with food, the food which was "in the mouth of Yitzchak." Yitzchak was convinced that Esav would do the same for Yaakov.

Esav deceived his father into thinking this was so. How? This is answered by Rashi's second explanation – Esav asked questions about tithing. To whom would the tithes be given? To the Torah

---

17. Bereishis 23:2.
18. See Bamidbar 13:22.
19. Rashi on Bereishis 49:13.

scholar. The deceit involved with these questions is trapping "in the mouth of Esav" – the words which Esav spoke.

The deception went further. Only food that grows in the ground and is fit for human consumption is liable to tithing.[20] Esav wanted to show that he was extra stringent, taking from straw which is not fit for human consumption and from salt which does not grow in the ground. That is why, to quote the Rashi mentioned above,

> *His father thought that he was meticulous in his performance of commandments.*

Straw is animal food. Esav was intimating that not only did he want to provide Yaakov with food, but he also wanted to take care of his possessions. The word for cattle, מקנה, is related to the root "possess," קנה. Therefore, giving straw to his animals is symbolic of concern for all his possessions.

What about salt? Salt is what gives taste to the food. Esav was implying that not only would he feed Yaakov, but that it would be more than just the basic essentials, it would be tasty.[21]

The proof that this was Yitzchak's vision is evident when he blesses Yaakov. Thinking that it is Esav whom he is blessing, the blessing refers to physical, rather than spiritual bounty:

---

20. Rambam, *Mishneh Torah, Hilchos Terumos* 2:1.
21. With this idea, we have a beautiful understanding of a comment Rashi makes on the story of Lot. When the city of Sodom was destroyed, Lot, his wife, and two unmarried daughters were saved. As they were fleeing, Lot's wife looked back, in spite of being told by the angel not to do so. The consequence was "she became a pillar of salt" (Bereishis 19:26). Rashi comments: "She sinned with salt and she was punished with salt. He [Lot] said to her, 'Give a little salt to these guests.' She replied, 'You even want to introduce that bad custom here!'" What is her antagonism to salt? She was maintaining that even though they were obliged to feed the guests, there was no need for the food to be tasty.

"G-d should give you from the dew of heaven and the fat of the earth, and an abundance of grain and wine."[22]

This abundance was intended to help support Yaakov. Rivkah realized that Yaakov could not be dependent on Esav, and arranged for Yaakov to receive the blessing of physical plenty.

To his *father*, Yitzchak, Esav was a dedicated son. Rivkah, though, knew that he could not be trusted to care for his *brother*.

12.5 AFTER THE BLESSING

When Esav discovers that Yaakov has received the blessing,

He cried out an exceedingly great and bitter scream. He said to his father, "Bless me too, my father."[23]

When Yitzchak explains that it is too late,

Esav said to his father, "Do you have only one blessing, my father? Bless me too, my father."[24]

Notice that Esav is constantly referring to his "father."

After this, when he decides he will kill Yaakov,

Esav said to himself, "Soon the days of mourning for my father will be here; then I will kill my brother, Yaakov."[25]

The *Yalkut Shimoni* comments:

Rebbe Yehudah taught: "Esav acted with calm calculation. He said, 'Why should I trouble Father? Soon the days of mourning for my father will be here.'"

---

22. Bereishis 27:28.
23. Ibid., v. 34.
24. Ibid., v. 38.
25. Ibid., v. 41.

Esav will not murder his brother while Yitzchak is alive. He does not want to pain his father. Once Yitzchak is dead, however, Yaakov can be slain.

12.6 "I WILL SUPPLANT YOU"

We have seen the danger of Lavan – the disconnection from roots.[26] What is the danger of Esav?

Esav tries to supplant Yaakov. Esav is so connected to his father that Yaakov is displaced. As we saw,

> *Yitzchak loved Esav because prey was in his mouth, but Rivkah loved Yaakov.*[27]

The clear implication is that Yitzchak loved Esav more than he loved Yaakov.

Lavan tries to sever all connections; Esav tries to supplant.

12.7 HONORING PARENTS CAN KILL YOU

When Yaakov flees the wrath of his brother, Esav sends his son Elifaz after Yaakov. Although there is no explicit mention of this in the Torah narrative, Chazal reveal it. Elifaz, son of Esav, pursued him in order to kill him, as commanded by his father. Since Elifaz had been raised close to Yitzchak, he restrained himself.

> *He said to him [Yaakov], "What do I do about the directive of my father?" Yaakov responded, "Take everything I have, because a poor man is considered as dead."*[28]

---

26. Sections 2.4, 2.7.
27. Bereishis 25:28.
28. *Nedarim* 64b.

Elifaz is a true son of Esav. Honoring his father is such a supreme value that he even contemplates killing Yaakov in order to fulfill his father's command.

Not only is Esav connected to his father, but his son is connected to him, following in his path. This is the exact opposite of Lavan, who was disconnected from both father and sons.

Lavan is dangerous from one direction, Esav from the other.

An idea which can give insights into portions of the Torah is that the *name* of the weekly *parshah* (Torah-reading) often has significance which shed light on that which occurs in that *parshah*.

It is interesting to note that the weekly Torah portion which recounts much of the story of Esav is called *Toldos*, which means "generations." This is an appropriate title for the section which discusses the story of Esav, a man connected to father and sons. The portion which recounts the story of Lavan is called *Veyetzei*, which means "and he left," referring to the departure of Yaakov from his father's home, not to return until the following *parshah*. Again, we have an appropriate title.

12.8 WHY IS YAAKOV AFRAID?

When Esav approaches Yaakov with four hundred armed men,

> *Yaakov was very afraid and distressed.*[29]

Why was he afraid? Chazal answer this question in a Midrash:

> *He [Yaakov] said, "All these years he [Esav] has been living in the land of Israel. Perhaps he can overcome me with the merit of living in Israel. All these years he has been able to honor his*

29. Bereishis 32:8.

> *parents. Perhaps he can overcome me with the merit of honoring father and mother."*[30]

How does the Midrash know that these were the reasons for Yaakov's fear?

When the Almighty told Yaakov to leave the home of Lavan and return home,

> *Hashem said to Yaakov, "Return to the* ***land*** *of your* ***fathers*** *and your birthplace, and I will be with you."*[31]

The emphasis is on "land" and "fathers," with an assurance of divine protection. The message is not to fear the merits of Esav regarding "land" and "fathers."

Once again, we see the threat to Yaakov from the honor that Esav has for parents.

12.8 ESAV IS WELL-RED

Having learned about the connection of Esav to his father, how does this shed light on his name, "Edom," meaning "red"?

Why is he born with red hair?

Why does he eat red lentils?

We asked these questions at the outset of our investigation.[32] Now we will answer them. In order to do so, we need to examine the red liquid.

---

30. *Bereishis Rabbah* 76:2.
31. Bereishis 31:3.
32. Sections 1.4, 1.5.

13

Blood relationships

13.1 BLOOD – LIQUID OF LIFE

As we have seen, the *Sefer Hachinuch* explained the command to honor parents: they gave us life and, therefore, it is incumbent upon us to show them gratitude.[1]

The symbol of life is blood. The Torah explains the reason for the prohibition to eat blood as follows:

> *This is because the life force of the flesh is in the blood; and I therefore gave it to you to be upon the altar to atone for your lives.*[2]

Rashi explains:

> *"Because the life force of the flesh" – Of every creature, is dependent on blood. Therefore I gave it to you to be upon the altar to atone for the life of man. Let "life" come and atone for "life."*[3]

---

1. Section 10.4.
2. Vayikra 17:11.
3. It is interesting to note that there is a Talmudic principle that anything

Blood circulates, bringing life to every part of the body. It is the archetypal symbol of life.

That is why when we speak about connections to family, to those who gave us life, we call them "blood relationships."

13.2 CREATION OF MAN – 1 PLUS 3 PLUS 41 EQUALS 45

Knowing this, we can appreciate a famous teaching of Chazal:

> *There are three partners in [the creation of] a man* (באדם)*: the Holy One, Blessed is He, his father and his mother.*[4]

The *Ben Ish Chai*, in his classic commentary on the aggadic portions of Talmud, *Ben Yehoyoda*, illuminates this teaching. The word used for "man" is אדם. The first letter of the word is *aleph*, the numerical value of which is "one." This represents the Holy One, Blessed is He, who is the Oneness of the world. The last two letters are דם which have a numerical value of 44. This is the same as the combined value of אב meaning "father," and אם meaning "mother."[5]

---

offered up as a sacrifice on the altar must be permissible for human consumption. (*Chullin* 90b) If so why are blood and *chelev*, forbidden fats, offered on the altar? Rashi, ad loc. s.v. *midi* explains that the principle only requires that the animal not be unkosher, but that any of the "meat," including the blood and fats can be offered. The question remains, *why* is this so? If blood may not be eaten, why is it offered? In fact the obligation to bring a sacrifice of an animal or bird has not been fulfilled if its blood has not been placed on the altar.

R. Moshe Feinstein, *zt"l* (*Dorash Moshe, Acharei Mos*) answered that the prohibition to eat blood is because it is too important for human consumption. As such, it is not rendered invalid for use to achieve atonement on the altar. Generally, the reason why something which is not permissible for human consumption is invalid as a sacrifice is because it is not good enough; in the case of blood, it is too good to be eaten. (The question remains why *chelev*, forbidden fats, *are* offered up on the altar. J.T.)

4. *Kiddushin* 30b.
5. אב = 1+2 = 3. אם = 1+40 = 41. 3+41 = 44 = דם.

The letter *aleph* is a letter connoting spirituality. It is the first letter, implying original source. It has no sound of its own, merely being a vehicle for the vowel placed with it. This lack of sound implies an element of concealment. The *aleph* in the word אדם represents the spiritual component, the soul, given by the Holy One, Blessed is He.

The last letters דם, "blood," represent the physical life force, which is contributed by the father and mother. That is why the sum of "father" (אב) and "mother" (אם) is the same as "blood" (דם).[6]

Again, we see that blood is the symbol of our relationship with our parents.

13.3 THE BLOODY BIRTH OF A NATION

Not just on an individual level, but also on a national level, blood is a crucial component in creation.

The exodus from Egypt is considered to be the birth of the nation.

> *"Has a god ever tried to take* ***a nation out of the midst of another nation****, with trials, signs and wondrous feats, and with war, a strong hand, an outstretched arm, and fearful deeds, like all which Hashem your G-d did for you in Egypt, in your sight?"*[7]

The Midrash, explains the phrase "a nation out of the midst of another nation," as meaning,

> *Like a baby being pulled out of the womb of its mother.*[8]

---

6. See *Niddah* 31b where the Talmud attributes the different parts of a child's body, some to the father and others to the mother. Blood is considered to be from the mother. This does not necessarily contradict the teaching of the *Ben Yehoyoda*, since "blood," besides being *part* of the body, is a symbol of the life-force as a *whole*, as we saw in section 13.1.
7. Devarim 4:34.
8. *Midrash Tehillim* 107:4.

Rashi, commenting on the commandment to sacrifice a Pesach lamb, writes:

> *Rabbi Masya son of Charash taught, "The verse says, 'I passed over you and I saw you. Behold your time, the time of affection, has arrived.' (Yechezkel 16:8) This refers to the oath which I swore to Avraham that I would redeem his children. But they did not have any commandments with which they were occupied. So I gave them two commandments, the* ***blood*** *of the Pesach sacrifice, and the* ***blood*** *of circumcision. They performed circumcision that night, as it says, '[I saw you] wallowing in your* ***bloods****' (ibid., v. 6), in two bloods."*[9]

The birth of the Jewish people is accompanied by two bloods, the blood of circumcision and the blood of the Pesach sacrifice.[10] These two commandments are central to being part of the nation.[11]

So blood is crucial at the birth of the individual and at the birth of the nation.

---

9. Shemos 12:6.
10. The reader is strongly recommended to read the wonderful essay by R. Mordechai Kornfeld called "The Seven Liquids and the Seven Moadim." In this essay, the author shows that the seven liquids which "prepare" food to receive ritual impurity (*Machshirin* 6:4) correspond to the seven festivals. In a nutshell: blood is the liquid of Pesach, as we have seen. Milk corresponds to Shavuot. Water corresponds to Sukkot. Honey corresponds to Rosh Hashanah. Dew, a symbol for repentance (see Hoshea 14:2-6), corresponds to Yom Kippur. Wine corresponds to Purim and oil to Chanukah.
    It would be an interesting challenge for the reader to work out the correspondence between these seven festivals and the seven species for which the land of Israel is praised: wheat, barley, grapes, figs, pomegranates, olives and dates. (See Devarim 8:8.)
11. That is the reason why they are the only two positive commandments which receive the punishment of *kares*, "cutting off" from any connection with the destiny of the Jewish people.

13.4 GOOD FOR YOU AND FOR YOUR CHILDREN

Having seen that "blood" is the symbol of life and connection with parents, family and nation, it is not surprising to see the reward for one who appreciates the special nature of blood and does not eat it:

> *Do not eat it, in order that it will be* ***good for you and your sons after you****, when you do that which is right in the eyes of Hashem. However, when you have any sacred offerings and pledges, you must take them and come to the place that Hashem will choose. Then, when you prepare your burnt offerings, both the flesh and the* ***blood*** *shall be placed on the altar of Hashem your G-d. The* ***blood*** *of eaten sacrifices shall be poured on the altar of Hashem your G-d, and the flesh shall be eaten. Guard and listen to all these words which I command you* ***in order that it will be good for you and your sons after you*** *forever when you do that which is good and right in the eyes of Hashem your G-d.*[12]

This phrase, למען ייטב לך ולבניך אחריך, "in order that it will be good for you and your sons after you," occurs only twice in the Chumash.[13] Both are in the verses quoted here, and both are in connection with how we treat blood.

If you understand the importance of blood, the liquid of life and the symbol of connection to parents and family, then it will be "good for you and your sons after you."

---

12. Devarim 12:25-28.
13. Even a similar phrase occurs only one other time. Moshe exhorts the Jewish nation to obey the Almighty: "Keep his statutes and commandments, which I command you today, *that it will be good for you and your sons after you.*" (Devarim 4:40) There the context is keeping the whole corpus of Torah. The only specific subject where we find the phrase is that of blood. Furthermore, Devarim 4 uses the word אשר and not למען.

13.5 ESAV'S COLOR IS RED

Red is the color of blood. In Hebrew, the connection is even deeper. The word for "red" is אדום. The very root of the word is דם, blood.

It is now clear why Esav's color is red. He is outstanding in his connection to his father. Therefore, at his birth, we are told,

> *The first twin was born red* (אדמוני), *completely covered with hair like a hairy coat and they called him Esav.*[14]

His external color mirrors his essential internal nature.

Why is he not called "Edom" (red) at birth? It is only after he sells his rights as firstborn that he receives the name Edom:

> *Yaakov was preparing a dish when Esav came back from the field exhausted. Esav said to Yaakov, "Pour down my throat now*[15] *from this red stuff* (מן האדם האדם הזה), *for I am exhausted" – therefore he is called Edom* (אדום).[16]

What does this mean?

Rashi explains:

> *"From this red stuff" – Red lentils. That day Avraham had died... and Yaakov was cooking lentils as food for mourners. Why lentils? They are round like a wheel; mourning is like a wheel which keeps rolling around again in the world.*

This was no regular food. This food showed connection to a grandfather who had passed away. We now understand why this is the food which Esav is eating.

Why is the emphasis in the verse on the fact that the lentils were red rather than round? Because red is the color of blood – the color of connection to family!

---

14. Bereishis 25:25.
15. See section 1.4 regarding the translation of the Hebrew word נא as "now."
16. Bereishis 25:29-30.

This connection to blood, if abused, can lead to violence and the shedding of blood. Indeed, Esav does become a murderer.[17] All characteristics can be used or misused.

When Esav was born, he already had this trait of "redness," but only in the form of potential. It is when he actualizes this trait, taking red lentils, that he acquires the name "Edom."

We have seen:

- Esav is a man who honors and is connected to his father.
- Blood, the liquid of life, represents our connection to our parents, who gave us life.
- As such, the color which represents Esav is red, the color of blood.
- We now understand why "Edom" becomes a name of Esav.
- This takes place after he eats the *red* lentils, the food of mourning for Avraham, indicating connection to family.

We still need to discover why Lavan is "white."

17. See Rashi on Bereishis 25:29.

14

Faces, roosters and twigs

14.1 WHEN BLOOD DRAINS AWAY

We have seen why Esav is called "Edom" (red).

Why is the evil Lavan called "white"?

The Mishnah in Avos states:

> *Rabbi Elazar Hamodai taught: "... One who embarrasses his friend in public... even though he has to his credit Torah study and good deeds, has no portion in the World to Come."*[1]

The phrase "embarrasses his friend in public" is a translation of והמלבין פני חברו ברבים. A literal translation would be "one who makes his friend's face white in public."

Why is this phrase used for embarrassment? Rashi comments:

> *Because the red goes and the white comes.*

When a person is embarrassed, initially his face turns red. Then the blood drains from his face which then becomes white.

When there is no blood, the color is white!

---

1. *Avos* 3:11.

Is there a more appropriate name for Lavan, a man totally detached from parents and family, than "white"? He has no connection to "blood." All that is left is "white"! That is the reason he is called לבן – white.

14.2 A WHITE-COMBED CHICKEN ON ONE LEG

Now that we know why Lavan is "white"[2] and that he is, in essence, Bilam,[3] we can better understand a very cryptic section of Talmud:

> *It was taught in a braisa, "G-d is angered every day,"[4] and how long does his anger last? A moment. How long is this "moment"? One fifty-eight thousand, eight hundred and eighty-eighth part of an hour. No creature can determine precisely when this moment occurs except for Bilam, the evil one [and he planned to curse the Jews at that moment of anger]...*
>
> *When does He become angry? During the first three hours of the day, when the comb of a rooster becomes white, and it stands on one leg.*
>
> *But at many other times it stands like this [i.e., on one leg with a white comb]?*
>
> *At all other times there are red streaks in it; at that time [the moment of G-d's anger], there are no red streaks in it.*[5]

This seems baffling.

There are a number of questions which present themselves:

1. If there is a visible sign, why is it true that, "No creature can determine precisely when this moment occurs except for Bilam, the evil one" – surely anyone can see the sign?

---

2. Since לבן, "white," is an absence of blood, the symbol of connection to parents. This is the essence of Lavan.
3. Bilam, like Lavan, tries to disconnect from parents.
4. Tehillim 7:12.
5. *Berachos* 7a.

2. Why is the sign connected to a "rooster"?
3. Why is it standing on "one leg"?
4. Why is the "comb" significant?
5. Why is the sign that the comb "becomes white" with "no red streaks in it"?

The first question is answered by the *Eitz Yosef* commentary on the *Ein Yaakov*.[6] Bilam was able to ascertain the moment even without a rooster, which no one else can do. He noticed that this moment coincided with the sign of the rooster standing on one leg with no red streaks in its comb. He realized that this sign was an indication of the moment of G-d's anger and revealed this to the world. Now, others can also determine the moment.

The rooster is often a symbol for man and human intelligence. One of the words for "man" is גבר. For example,

> *Happy is the man* (הגבר) *who places his trust in Hashem.*[7]

The same word is used to mean rooster.[8] Discussing the morning Temple service, the Mishnah teaches,

---

6. The *Ein Yaakov* is a compendium of the aggadic sections of the Talmud.
7. Tehillim 40:5.
8. Not only does the word גבר mean both "man" and "rooster," but the word שכוי has a similar double meaning:
   The Talmud teaches: When one hears the crowing of a rooster [in the morning], one should say, "Blessed is He ... who gives understanding to the rooster (לשכוי) to distinguish between day and night." (*Berachos* 60b)
   The *Shulchan Aruch* (*O.H.* 46:1) quotes this and the *Mishnah Berurah* (46:4), quoting the Rosh, comments:
   > "To the rooster (לשכוי) – the heart is called שכוי, as it says, "Or who gave understanding to the heart (לשכוי)." (Iyov 38:36) The heart is that which understands and, with this understanding, a man can distinguish between day and night. Since a rooster can also understand this and, since man benefits from hearing it, knowing that day-break is near, and since in Arabic a rooster is called שכוי, the Rabbis enacted this blessing on hearing the crow of the rooster."

   The Rosh interprets the blessing to mean "who gives understanding to the *heart* (לשכוי) to distinguish between day and night."

Every day they would remove ash from the altar when the rooster crowed (בקריאת הגבר) or slightly before or after.[9]

The comparison is clearest in the custom to take *kaparos*. The day before Yom Kippur, there is a custom is to take a rooster for each man[10] and to say certain verses. The rooster is then slaughtered in place of the man, atoning for his sins.[11] The reason that the rooster is used for this custom is based on the linguistic parallel we have seen.

Why "standing on one leg"?

The leg is the symbol of the "son." A famous idea in Jewish law is ברא כרעא דאבוה, i.e., "the son is the leg of his father."[12] When the father can no longer move, the son carries on going in his place.

We see this idea in the fight that Yaakov has prior to his meeting with Esav:

Yaakov remained alone. A man struggled with him until morning. When he saw that he could not prevail he touched the hollow of [Yaakov's] thigh. The hollow of Yaakov's thigh was put out of joint as he wrestled with him.[13]

Who was the stranger who assaulted Yaakov? Rashi, quoting the Midrash, reveals:

Rashi (*Berachos* 60b) and Avudraham (*Birchos Hashachar*) disagree with the Rosh. They interpret the blessing according to the straightforward reading of the quote from the Talmud: "who gives understanding to the *rooster* (לשכוי) to distinguish between day and night."

Thus the word for rooster is identical to a word meaning human intelligence.

9. *Yoma* 1:8.
10. A chicken is used for a woman.
11. See *Shulchan Aruch* and Rema, *O.H.* 605. Today, many give money instead of using roosters and chickens.
12. See, for example, Rebbe Akiva Eiger, *Teshuvos Hachadoshim* 39 and *Chidushei Rebbe Akiva Eiger, Bava Kama* 112a. See *Eiruvin* 70b and *Shulchan Aruch O.C.* 381:6 which suggest that the original phrase was יורש כרעי' דאבוה.
13. Bereishis 32:25-26.

> *He was the spiritual force representing Esav.*

What is the idea conveyed by the attack on the leg of Yaakov? The Midrash explains:

> *"He touched the hollow of [Yaakov's] thigh" – These are the righteous men and women, prophets and prophetesses that were destined to be his descendants.*[14]

The leg represents the future descendants of a person.

If we return to Lavan, we see the theme of רגל appearing there as well.

We have seen[15] that Lavan, when trying to persuade Yaakov to stay with him after fourteen years, admitted that it was only in the merit of Yaakov that he had merited fathering sons.

Yaakov, in response to Lavan's request to remain with him, says:

> *"Hashem has blessed you because of my coming* (לרגלי)*; now when can I also provide for my household?"*[16]

The use of the word לרגלי to mean "my coming" is unusual.

If a word is used, which is not the normal word for the idea, the reason should be investigated.

The Ibn Ezra explains the word to mean "for me," also an unusual use of the word.

---

14. *Bereishis Rabbah* 77:3. Although Esav is connected to his own father and son, he wants to replace Yaakov as the primary son of Yitzchak, and tries to destroy Yaakov and his future descendants.
15. Section 7.2.
16. Bereishis 30:30. Rashi on this verse provides a further insight into the close connection which Yaakov has with his sons. Rashi is bothered by the use of the word "also," and comments: "Also provide for my household" – For the needs of my household. At present it is only my *sons* who are providing for my needs; I also need to provide together with them, to back them up – that is [the meaning of] "also."

Based on what we have now learned, it seems that Yaakov is using a word that alludes to connection with children, and is implying, "only because of my connection to children were you blessed with sons!"

We know[17] that Bilam is trying to sever the connection between fathers and sons. The rooster, a symbol for man, is standing only on one leg. The stability is not what it should be. The symbolic continuity indicated by "legs" is deficient.

We asked why is the sign that the comb "becomes white" with "no red streaks in it"?

The rooster's comb, on top of its head, is an indication of what is on its mind. The moment that the comb turned totally white, without a streak of red, was an indication that Bilam could achieve success with a curse. The curse would be to implant total disconnection from parents into the mind of the Jews. This is Lavan/Bilam in action!

14.3 WHITE STICKS

Perhaps the most remarkable example of "Lavan," disconnection from parents, in action is Lavan against Lavan. We know that after fourteen years working for Lavan in order to marry Rachel, Yaakov wanted to return to his father's home.

Lavan agreed that Yaakov's wages would be sheep and goats with very specific markings. Yaakov was not given any sheep or goats to shepherd with those markings. So what would happen if the children born to the animals he was given would resemble their parents? Yaakov would receive no payment at all![18]

---

17. See chapter 3.
18. See section 7:13 where this is discussed in detail.

However, this is not what happened. The lambs and kids are born with the markings that are to be the payment of Yaakov. When the children differ from their parents, it is Lavan who loses!

Now we can examine how this was achieved. How did Yaakov ensure that the children would not resemble the fathers?

ויקח לו יעקב מקל **לבנה** לח ולוז וערמון ויפצל בהן פצלות **לבנות** מחשף **הלבן** אשר על המקלות:

Yaakov took moist sticks of poplar (**לבנה**)*, almond and plane. He peeled* ***white*** *streaks in them, uncovering the* ***white*** *layer of the sticks.*[19]

Yaakov takes a number of different types of branches. One is called לבנה, from the root לבן, "white." It has white bark. The others, "almond and plane," do not have white bark. The bark is peeled from these branches, revealing the white layer (הלבן) underneath. Now they all look white.

He set up the sticks that he peeled in the watering troughs, when the flocks came to drink, facing the animals. They mated when they came to drink. The flocks mated in the presence of the sticks, and gave birth to young which were ringed, spotted and streaked.[20]

Yaakov ensured that the young would not resemble their fathers by showing them לבן. When the sheep see this, their young will not look like them. As a result, Yaakov keeps the offspring.

Lavan is totally defeated by לבן. Astonishing!

---

19. Bereishis 30:37.
20. Ibid., vv. 38-39.

15

"Let Dad sleep!"

15.1 DAMA BEN NESINAH

We have seen that "red" and "stones" both represent connection to parents. We might expect to find them connected in other Torah sources which discuss how we relate to our parents. Is this so?

Let us examine a famous story in the Talmud:

> *Rav Yehudah said in the name of Shmuel: They asked R' Eliezer: "How far does the commandment to honor parents extend?" He answered them: "Go and see what one idolator did for his father in Ashkelon, and his name was Dama son of Nesinah.*
> *The Sages wanted to buy stones for the ephod,*[1] *giving him a profit of six hundred gold dinars. Rav Cahana taught that the potential profit was eight hundred thousand.*
> *The key to the chest [that contained the precious stones] was under his father's pillow [and his father was sleeping]. He did not disturb him [and as a result did not make the sale].*

1. The question whether the stones were actually for the *ephod* garment, or for the *choshen* breastplate, will be clarified in section 15.3.

"Let Dad sleep!"

> *The following year, the Holy One, Blessed is He, gave him his reward, that a 'parah adumah' (red cow) was born in his herd. The Sages went to him [to purchase it].*
> *He said to them: 'I know you, that if I would ask from you all the money in the world, you would give it to me. However, I ask from you only the amount of money that I lost as a result of honoring my father.'"*[2]

There are a number of questions that present themselves upon reading this story:

Why do we learn how to honor parents from an idolator? Is there no Jew worthy of emulation in this area?

Why do we need to be told his name – "Dama son of Nesinah"?

Why are we told from where he came – "Ashkelon"?

Why is it significant that he was selling "stones for the ephod"?

Would his father not want to be woken when such a huge profit is at stake?

Why is his reward a *"parah adumah"*?

To answer these questions, we need to distinguish between different types of commandments.

15.2 STATUTES AND JUDGMENTS

There are two different categories of commandment that are often mentioned in juxtaposition in the Torah: חקים, translated as "statutes," and משפטים, translated as "judgments." What is the difference between the two? One of the verses in which they are mentioned together says:

> *You shall do my judgments, and keep my statutes, to walk in them. I am Hashem your G-d.*[3]

---

2. *Kiddushin* 31a, *Avodah Zarah* 23b-24a.
3. Vayikra 18:4.

Rashi comments:

> *"You shall do my judgments" – These are matters which are justly mentioned in the Torah, such that even if they would not have been said, it would have been appropriate to enact them.*
> *"And keep my statutes" – Matters which are the King's decree. The evil inclination retorts concerning them, "Why do we need to observe them?" And the idolatrous nations of the world retort concerning them.*
> *They include [not] eating pig, [nor] wearing sha'atnez, ritual purity by means of water containing ashes of the parah adumah. Therefore the verse continues, "I am Hashem your G-d," i.e., "It is My decree, you are not permitted to exempt yourselves."*

The idolatrous nations can understand and appreciate a "judgment." This includes many of the prohibitions of the Torah, such as murder, theft and adultery. These are commandments that the human mind can comprehend.

However, a "statute" is beyond human comprehension. Although we can suggest possible rationales, they are no more than suggestions. Therefore, the evil inclination and the nations of the world taunt us for observing them.

Our response is that our observance is not dependent on our comprehension. If that were so, then we would be in charge. It is the Almighty who is in charge. He commands and we obey.

Besides those negative commands that even the nations of the world can comprehend, there are certain positive commands that they can appreciate. Perhaps the best example is the commandment to respect parents.

The concept that it is right to show parents respect, out of gratitude for all they have done for their children, is patently obvious. Even idolators can relate to this.

15.3 RED NAME, RED STONE

We can now study the name of this very respectful son, who is an idol worshipper.

The name "Dama" (דמא) is from the Hebrew word דם, meaning "blood." Blood is the life force of the human body, and is the symbol of what our parents have given us. Dama appreciates that his parents have given him life.

He is "son of Nesinah" (בן נתינה), which means "son of giving." He understands that he owes gratitude for what he has received from his parents.

The name of his town is "Ashkelon" (אשקלון), which is related to the word לשקול, to weigh. Dama weighs up what he has received and feels obliged to *balance* this out by giving back in return. It is a *quid pro quo* relationship.

What is his profession? He sells *stones*! They are precious stones. He values the אב–בן bond.

The Sages want to buy his stones "for the *ephod*." The *ephod* was a garment worn by the High Priest. It had shoulder straps from which the breastplate, with its twelve stones, was suspended. Each shoulder strap had a precious stone, and on each stone was engraved the names of six of Yaakov's sons.[4]

It would seem, therefore, that the Sages went to purchase the two stones for the *ephod*. Tosfos[5] proves that this cannot have been so, that the stones were really for the breastplate which hung from the *ephod*. A proof that this is so is that the version of this story in the Talmud Yerushalmi[6] recounts that it was one of the stones of the breastplate that was lost, and the Sages went to buy a replacement. Which stone was it? It was the stone of Binyamin, ישפה, the last of the

---

4. Shemos 28:6-12.
5. *Avodah Zarah* 24a.
6. *Peah* 3a, *Kiddushin* 20a.

twelve stones mentioned in the command to make the breastplate.[7]

The breastplate of the High Priest had twelve precious stones, each with one of the names of the twelve tribes.[8] The High Priest could ask questions and receive answers from the Almighty. The answers were transmitted by means of the engraved letters lighting up or standing out.

The Talmud points out that not all the letters of the *aleph-beis* are contained in the names of the tribes. Where was the letter *tzaddi*?[9] The answer is that the names of the forefathers were also engraved on the stones – אברהם יצחק יעקב, and, thereby, *tzaddi* was also included. What about the letter *tes*? The phrase שבטי ישורון, *"tribes of Yeshurun,"*[10] was also engraved.[11]

So these stones really represent the idea of אב–בן, with all the fathers included, and the names of the tribes, their descendants.

It is thus appropriate that the purchase of a stone for this breastplate is from a man who values the father-son relationship.

Why, according to the Talmud Yerushalmi, was it specifically the stone of Binyamin that the Sages were going to purchase?

The *Meshech Chochmah*[12] gives a beautiful explanation:

We know that Yosef's brothers sold him into slavery. Yaakov thought that Yosef had been devoured by a wild animal.

> *Yaakov tore his robes in grief and put on sackcloth. He mourned for his son for many days.*[13]

---

7. Shemos 28:20.
8. Ibid., vv. 17-21.
9. The *Tosfos Yeshanim*, ad loc., points out that the letters *ches* and *kuf* are also absent from the names of the tribes. They are included in the name יצחק, and thus the answer given for the absence of *tzaddi* will answer the absence of these letters as well.
10. Another name for Yisrael, the Jewish people (see Devarim 32:15).
11. *Yoma* 73b.
12. Shemos 28:9.
13. Bereishis 37:34.

We have seen[14] Rashi's comment:

> *"Many days" – Twenty-two years, from when [Yosef] was separated from him until Yaakov went down to Egypt [to be reunited with Yosef].*

So the brothers caused their father great pain and anguish, and were remiss in the fulfillment of the commandment to honor their father.

Yosef, too, was instrumental in the pain of his father. For the entire twenty-two years, he never sent a message to his father that he was still alive.

Binyamin, though, was not involved in the sale. He was the one brother that was not included in the failure to show respect to Yaakov. In fact his name, בנימין, starts with the word בן. His essence is that he is a *son*.

It is *his* stone that the Sages wish to buy from Dama son of Nesinah.

What stone was it? ישפה. Chazal reveal why this was the stone of Binyamin:

> ישפה – *This is a contraction of* יש פה, *"there is a mouth." Although Binyamin knew about the sale of Yosef, he said nothing.*[15]

Although he has a mouth, Binyamin says nothing, because, if he revealed what he knew, it would create a rift between *father and sons*!

What type of stone is ישפה? The word is a cognate of the English "jasper."

In the entry defining "jasper" the Random House Webster's Unabridged Dictionary writes:

---

14. Section 5.1.
15. *Bereishis Rabbah* 71:5.

Jasper – a compact, opaque, cryptocrystalline variety of quartz, usually colored red.

What could be more fitting for the man who is the exemplar of respect for and connection to parents than a *red stone*?

It is remarkable to quote what Rabbeinu Bechaye says about this stone. Every one of the stones had special properties. What is the special property of the stone of Binyamin?

Its special property is that it stops bleeding.[16]

It is not surprising that the stone of Binyamin, which *Dama* ben Nesinah possesses, prevents loss of blood. Binyamin, who exemplifies honoring parents, has a stone which ensures that blood is not lost!

15.4 THE ABC OF WOLVES

The blessing which Binyamin receives from his father is most appropriate in the light of what we have learned about Binyamin:

Binyamin is a ravaging wolf (זאב)*. In the morning he shall devour the prey, and in the evening he shall divide the spoil.*[17]

Is being a "wolf" a blessing?

The Midrash[18] interprets the verse as alluding to the altar in the Temple, which was built in the portion of Binyamin:

R' Pinchas explained the verse as relating to the altar. Just as the wolf seizes, so too the altar seizes sacrifices. "In the morning he shall devour the prey" refers to "one lamb you shall prepare in the morning";[19] *"and in the evening he shall divide*

16. Rabbeinu Bechaye on Shemos 28:15.
17. Bereishis 49:27.
18. *Bereishis Rabbah* 99:3.
19. Bamidbar 28:4.

> *the spoil" refers to "and the second lamb you shall prepare in the evening."*[20]

The two lambs are the daily *tamid* offering of the community, one in the morning and one in the evening.

This is the midrashic explanation.

According to the *pshat,* the straightforward reading, why is Binyamin compared to a wolf?

We need to learn about wolves. An expert on wolves, in an anonymous article called "The Wolf Pack,"[21] writes (my emphasis):

> *Wolves are an extremely social animal. They exist as a social unit called a pack. Wolves hunt and travel in a group and perform almost all other activities in the company of fellow wolves.*
>
> *The pack, the basic unit of wolf social life, is usually a* ***family group****. It is made up of animals related to each other by* ***blood*** *and* ***family ties*** *of affection and mutual aid.*
>
> *The core of a pack is a mated pair of wolves – an adult male and female that have bred and produced young. The other members of the pack are their offspring: young wolves ranging in age from pups to two and three-year-olds.*
>
> *Individual wolves in a pack play different roles in relation to others in the group. The* ***parent*** *wolves are the* ***leaders*** *of the pack – the alpha male and the alpha female.*[22] *[Alpha is the first letter in the Greek alphabet.] The alpha male and female are the oldest members of the pack and the ones with the most experience in hunting, defending territory, and other important activities.*

20. Ibid.
21. See "Wolf Web – Home of Wolves."
22. It is noteworthy that the words אב and אם both start with the letter *aleph*.

> *The other pack members* ***respect*** *their position in almost all things. The alpha wolves are usually the ones to make decisions for the pack when the group should go out to hunt or move from one place to another.*

Wolves are the animals which excel in respect for parents! The wolf is the animal most like Binyamin.

We know that one word is often to be understood as a contraction of two or more words or ideas.

We have seen that אבן is a contraction of אב–בן and that לבן is a contraction of לא בן. What is the meaning of זאב, "wolf"? The Midrash gives an answer which is amazing, although not unexpected:

> *"Binyamin is a ravaging wolf* (זאב)*" –* זאב *stands for* זה אב*, "this is father" to the entire Jewish nation. Just as sons gather together with their father, so too, the Jewish nation gathers [at the Temple, in the portion of Binyamin] the entire year round.*[23]

In the merit of flawless respect for his father, the Temple is built in the portion of Binyamin. This is the center of the "pack."

Now both the straightforward interpretation of "wolf," that it refers to Binyamin, is very much connected to the midrashic interpretation that it refers to the altar. In the merit of outstanding respect for his father, Binyamin merits that the altar, the focus of the "pack," is built in his portion.

The stones of the breastplate are where the names of the "pack members" come together as a prerequisite for the service of the High Priest in the Temple.

It is now beautifully appropriate that it is the *red stone* of Binyamin, the *wolf*, which is being sought from Dama son of Nesina.

---

23. *Bereishis Rabbasi* on Bereishis 49:27. This work of *midrash* is based mainly on the writings of R. Moshe Hadarshan, who is often quoted by Rashi in his commentary on Chumash.

15.5 "WHY DIDN'T YOU WAKE ME UP?"

Why does the Talmud not give a Jew as the exemplar of respect for parents?

Let us examine the dilemma of Dama ben Nesinah. If he does not wake his father, he stands to lose a huge profit.

The Talmud[24] discusses who has to pay for the respect to parents. For example, if the father wants a drink, does the son need to pay for the purchase, or is it at the father's expense?

The halachic decision in the *Shulchan Aruch* states:

> *When a child gives a parent food or drink, the cost is paid by the parent if he has money.*[25]

Since Dama does not need to lose money for respecting his father, why can he not wake his father?

Some commentators answer that a son does not need to spend money to *honor* parents, but he is not allowed to *pain* them, and in order to avoid this he is obliged to spend all his money.[26]

Another answer is that the son does not need to *spend* his own money to honor a parent, but he is obliged to *forgo profit* to honor them.[27]

Even after these answers, it is still difficult to understand why Dama did not wake his father. The *Be'er Heitev*, in his commentary on *Shulchan Aruch*,[28] quotes *Sefer Chassidim*:[29]

> *One does not wake a father only if he would not be upset at not*

---

24. *Kiddushin* 32a.
25. *Y.D.* 240:5.
26. Ran, *Kiddushin* 32a (first answer); *Tosfos Harosh, Kiddushin* 31a (second answer).
27. Ran, *Kiddushin* 32a (second answer); *Tosfos Harosh, Kiddushin* 31a (first answer).
28. *Y.D.* 240:16
29. Para. 337.

being woken. If, however, the father would be very happy to be woken, it is a mitzvah to wake him.

How did Nesinah, Dama's father, feel on waking, to discover that a deal yielding a huge profit had been lost? Even if the stones belonged to Dama, is it not reasonable to presume that the father would be devastated at such a loss for his son? Would he not have wanted his son to wake him?

R. Moshe Feinstein[30] answers that one must say that the father was not of sound mind.

This is not straightforward. Although it is clear from the Talmud that Dama's mother was insane,[31] there is no such indication from any other source that his father was the same.

Perhaps an easier answer is based on the first question we asked: Why do we learn how to honor parents from an idolator? Is there no Jew worthy of emulation in this area?

The answer is that Dama was totally mistaken in not waking his father. Although his heart was in the right place, he was not directed by Torah. He was convinced that one never wakes a parent unless, perhaps, the parent has requested to be woken.[32]

So why is he brought as an exemplar of respect for parents? To show how far one should be *prepared* to go. In his case, though, he was in error.

---

30. *Dibros Moshe, Kiddushin* Ch. 50, comment 17; *Igros Moshe, Y.D.* V 26:2.
31. See *Kiddushin* 31a, which recounts that Dama was dressed in gold-embroidered, silk clothing, sitting with the nobles of Rome. His mother came, tore his garment from him, hit him and spat in his face. From here it is clear that she was not of sound mind. The story is brought to show another example of Dama's respect for his parents. In spite of his public humiliation by his mother, he in no way retaliates. Tosfos, ad loc., s.v. *u'vos* quotes a *midrash* which explicitly says that she was insane.
32. This answer is also given by R. Chaim Kaniewski, as quoted in *Derech Sichah, parshas Yisro*, p. 290.

"Let Dad sleep!"

Support for this explanation can be found in the Talmud Yerushalmi's version of the story, which includes the following addition:

> *He [Dama] never sat on the stone on which his father sat. When his father died, he made it his object of worship.*[33]

Dama was fulfilling the rule we have learned:[34]

> *Fear [of a father] includes not standing in his place and not sitting in his place.*[35]

It is remarkable that this "seat" of Dama's father was a *stone*! There is no more appropriate object.

However, Dama does not have correct perspective, which is only obtained with Torah. For him, the stone becomes an idol!

Let us return to the first words of the story:

> *Rav Yehudah said in the name of Shmuel: They asked R' Eliezer: How far does the commandment to honor parents extend? He answered them: Go and see what one* ***idolator*** *did for his father in Ashkelon, and* ***his name was Dama son of Nesinah****.*

The idolatory is that he is "Dama son of Nesinah." He takes respect for parents out of all correct proportion. The stone of his father becomes an idol, and he will not rouse his father, even if it is the right thing to do.

15.6 RED COW

Why is the reward that Dama receives a red cow?

The *parah adumah* was used for ritual purification of those who had become impure as a result of contact with a dead body.

---

33. *Peah* 3a, *Kiddushin* 20a.
34. Section 10.6.
35. *Kiddushin* 31b.

The section of the Torah that details the laws of the *parah adumah* starts as follows:

> *G-d spoke to Moshe and Aharon saying, "This is a* ***statute*** *of the Torah which G-d commanded saying, 'Speak to the children of Israel. Let them bring you a totally red cow, which has no blemish, and which has never had a yoke on it.'"*[36]

The commandment of *parah adumah* is categorized as a statute. We saw[37] that when Rashi gives three examples of statutes, one of them is *parah adumah.*

In fact, it is the ultimate statute. Shlomo Hamelech, the wisest of all men said,

> *"I said I will be wise, but it is far from me."*[38]

The Midrash understands this verse as referring to *parah adumah*:

> *Shlomo said, "I comprehended all these [complicated laws], but the section of parah adumah, although I probed, asked and examined, I said I will be wise, but it is far from me."*[39]

Although it purifies the impure, those who are involved in burning the cow, gathering the ashes, placing them in water, sprinkling the water on the impure, all become impure!

It seems to be a commandment beyond human logic.

Dama ben Nesinah, an idolator, is capable of making great financial sacrifice for a judgment, something which the human mind can fathom and appreciate. In fact, his action could be a claim against the Jewish people: why do you not show such respect to your parents?

The Almighty, in His infinite kindness, demonstrated the greatness of the Jews through the reward which Dama receives. It is a *parah*

---

36. Bamidbar 19:1-2.
37. Section 15.2.
38. Kohelles 7:23.
39. *Bamidbar Rabbah* 19:3.

adumah, the ultimate statute. When the Sages come to purchase it, Dama, himself, says:

> *"I know you, that if I would ask from you all the money in the world, you would give it to me."*

Unlike idolators who only understand judgments, Jews are prepared to sacrifice everything even for a statute, and even for the most unfathomable of statutes.[40]

Although *parah adumah* is beyond human comprehension, there are insights and reasons which have been suggested. We have already seen the verses which introduce this commandment:

> *G-d spoke to Moshe and Aharon saying, "This is a statute of the Torah which G-d commanded saying, 'Speak to the children of Israel. Let them bring you a totally red cow, which has no blemish, and which has never had a yoke on it.'"*[41]

Why is a red cow used?

One of the tools often used by Rashi is that of *mashal* – a parable or analogy. The *nimshal*, moral or message, needs to be extracted.

Rashi expounds,[42] in the name of R. Moshe Hadarshan:

> *"Let them bring (literally, take) you" – Belonging to them. Just as they took off their own golden earrings for the golden calf, so too, they should bring this atonement from that which is their own.*
> *"Red cow" – This is understood with a mashal (analogy): The son of a maidservant dirtied the palace of the king. They said, "Let the mother clean up the mess." Similarly, let the cow come and atone for the calf.*

---

40. This explanation is given by the *Ben Yehoyada* on *Kiddushin* 31a, in the name of his son, R. Yaakov.
41. Bamidbar 19:1-2.
42. In his commentary following Bamidbar 19:22.

At the revelation on Sinai, the Jews were restored to the level of Adam, the first man, before he was tempted to sin.[43] Death could not prevail over them. However, as result of sinning with the golden calf, this level was lost, and now they would be subject to death.[44]

The spiritual blockage of impurity, caused by contact with death, was the result of the golden calf. The cow atones for the golden calf. The mother atones for her son.

Why, though, is the cow red?

Red is the color which represents connection between parents and children. The mother who comes to atone for her child is red.

It is perfectly fitting that the reward of the man so connected to parents, is the red cow, a symbol of a parent connected to child.

It is remarkable that perhaps the most famous Talmudic story about connection with, and respect for, a father contains the themes of "red" and "stones."

---

43. *Shabbos* 146a.
44. See *Ohr Hachayim*, Shemos 32:19.

16
Bilam's leg

16.1 BILAM'S LEG

A major theme which we have encountered is that of "stones" representing connection between fathers and sons.

Is it possible that a stone, the ultimate inanimate object, can have an active role in promoting this connection? In this chapter and the next, we will see that stones *can* play a very active role.

We have discovered that Bilam (alias Lavan) tries to disconnect the Jews from their Patriarchs.[1] We have also discovered how the Almighty punished Lavan using his own tactics against him.[2]

With this in mind, it is remarkable to see how Bilam is punished. We know that the angel blocked Bilam's path three times, and we have seen how these three occurences correspond to Avraham, Yitzchak and Yaakov.[3]

The second time the angel blocks the way, we read:

> *Hashem's angel then stood in a narrow path through the*

---

1. See chapter 3 and section 14.2.
2. Sections 7.12 and 7.13.
3. Section 3.8.

vineyards, with a fence on this side and a fence on that side. When the donkey saw Hashem's angel, she pressed herself against the wall, and she crushed Bilam's leg against the wall.[4]

Why is it his "leg" which is crushed? We have learned that the leg is the symbol of the "son."[5]

We now appreciate why it is Bilam's *leg* which is crushed. He is trying to disconnect the children, so the punishment is directed to his leg. The angel stands in three different places, to demonstrate to Bilam that the Almighty understood that he was trying to sever the link to the three fathers. So, too, the leg is crushed to show that the Almighty understood that it was the children being attacked.

It is fascinating to note that when the donkey speaks to Bilam and refers to the three times she had been hit, she says:

"What did I do to you that you hit me these three times?"[6]

The Hebrew word used for "times" is רגלים, connected to the word רגל, meaning "leg."

Then when the angel speaks to Bilam we read:

"Why did you hit your donkey these three times (רגלים)*?... The donkey saw me and turned away from me these three times* (רגלים)*..."*[7]

Three instances, in the space of six verses, the word רגלים is used to mean "times." These are the *only* occurrences in Tenach of this usage of the word רגלים with this meaning.

If a word is used with an unusual meaning in a small number of occurrences, there must be some significance.

---

4. Bamidbar 22:24-25.
5. See section 14.2.
6. Bamidbar 22:28.
7. Ibid., vv. 32-33.

Rashi comments:

> *"These three times (רגלים)" – [The donkey] was hinting to him: "You are trying to uproot a nation which celebrates three foot-festivals (רגלים) a year."*[8]

Why are there multiple references to the celebration of the foot-festivals, rather than any other commandment? One of the super-commentaries on Rashi, the *Tseidah Laderech*, explains:

> *The Patriarchs are the "legs" [i.e., supports] of the world.*[9]*... In addition, the Tur*[10] *teaches that the festival of Pesach corresponds to Avraham... Shavuos corresponds to Yitzchak... and Succos to Yaakov.*[11]

Therefore, not only does the triple location of the angel allude to the relationship with Patriarchs, but we also have the multiple-reference to רגלים, "legs," which again expresses our connection with our Fathers.

---

8. Rashi on Bamidbar 22:28.
9. See Rashi on Shemos 32:13, quoting *Berachos* 32a, which describes how Moshe responds to the Almighty's offer that, though He would destroy the Jewish nation following the sin of the golden calf, He would make a new nation from the descendants of Moshe: "If a chair with *three legs* cannot stand before You at a time of your anger, how much more so a chair with only one leg?" The "three legs" refer to the Patriarchs. Moshe argues that if the merits of the *three* Patriarchs cannot protect their descendants, then Moshe's descendants do not stand a chance.
   It is also relevant to mention the Mishnah (*Avos* 1:2): "The world *stands on three things*: on Torah on Avodah and on acts of kindness." As is well known, Avraham is the epitome of kindness, Yitzchak of Avodah, and Yaakov of Torah. (see *Gur Aryeh*, Bereishis 24:22)
10. *O.H.* 517.
11. See *Tseidah Laderech*, who quotes the scriptural inferences of the *Tur* for these parallels. Some explain that Shavuos corresponds to Yaakov and Sukkos to Yitzchak. See, for example, the commentary *Be'er Basadeh* on Rashi, Bamidbar 22:28.

16.2 FENCING OPPONENT

Perhaps the most incredible observation of Rashi in this story is a short, seemingly mundane comment.

When the angel comes the second time,

> *Hashem's angel then stood in a narrow path through the vineyards, with a fence on this side and a fence on that side.*[12]

Rashi comments:

> *"A fence on this side and a fence on that side" – The connotation of the word* גדר*, "fence," is that it was made of stones.*

Why do we need to know that the fence was made of stones?

The answer is fabulous. Bilam, alias Lavan or לא בן, is being broken by אבן! The man who is the antithesis of connection to parents is crushed by the very symbol of that connection. Amazing!

The remarkable nature of this crushing of Bilam goes further:

> *When the donkey saw Hashem's angel, she pressed herself* (וַתִּלָּחֵץ) *against the wall, and she crushed* (וַתִּלְחַץ) *Bilam's leg against the wall* (הַקִּיר)*.*[13]

Why does the word used for the pile of stones change in the same verse from גָּדֵר (fence) to הַקִּיר (the wall)?

Furthermore, the root לחץ, meaning "to press" or "to pressure," occurs twice in this verse. This root is unusual in Chumash and only occurs in four other verses, all of which share a common idea. We have seen numerous examples of the thematic connection of word roots which occur rarely.

---

12. Bamidbar 22:24.
13. Ibid., v. 25.

What is the common theme and how does it connect to the crushing of Bilam's leg?

All the other occurrences of the root לחץ refer to, or are related to, the oppression of the Jews by the Egyptians:

> *I have also seen the pressure* (הלחץ) *with which the Egyptians oppress* (לחצים) *them.*[14]
> *Hashem heard our voice and saw our affliction, our hard labor, and our oppression* (לחצנו).[15]

Having experienced being the oppressed foreigners in Egypt, we ourselves are commanded not to oppress strangers:

> *Do not hurt the feelings of a stranger or oppress* (ולא תלחצנו) *him, for you were strangers in the land of Egypt.*[16]
> *Do not oppress* (לא תלחץ) *a stranger; you know the feelings of a stranger for you were strangers in the land of Egypt.*[17]

So the root לחץ has the common theme of oppression of the Jews by the Egyptians.

What was the ultimate expression of this לחץ?

We have seen[18] how far the cruelty of the Egyptians went:

> *[If] any man was lacking one brick* (לבנה) *[from his daily quota], the Egyptians forcibly took his young boy... and placed him in the building in place of the brick.*[19]

How did Chazal derive that this occurred?

A similar Midrash is found in *Pirkei D' Rebbe Eliezer*:[20]

---

14. Shemos 3:9.
15. Devarim 26:7.
16. Shemos 22:20.
17. Ibid., 23:9.
18. Section 8.4.
19. *Sefer Hayashar*, (Tel Aviv, 1955) pp. 188-189.
20. Ch. 48. See also *Yalkut Shimoni, remez* 169.

The officers of Pharaoh smothered the Jews in the walls (בקירות) *of the houses, between the bricks* (הלבנים).

R. David Luria, the Redal, in his commentary to the *Pirkei D' Rebbe Eliezer*, explains how this was derived from the Torah text.

Firstly, we read in connection with the slavery in Egypt:

> ...ויאנחו בני ישראל מן העבדה ויזעקו ותעל שועתם אל האלהים מן העבדה:
>
> *The children of Yisrael groaned because of the work and they screamed; their cry rose up to G-d, because of the work.*[21]

It is an important grammatical tool to know that prepositions and prepositional-prefixes can have more than one meaning.

For example, the preposition ב can mean "in," "at" or "with."

In the verse we are examining, the preposition מן is used twice. English translations render these two instances as "because of."

In fact, the more literal meaning of the word is "from," i.e., "from the midst of."

The Redal explains that the Midrash is based on the literal meaning of מן:

"The children of Yisrael groaned *from* the work" – The children were groaning from the midst of the brickwork, having been used in place of bricks.

"Their cry rose up to G-d, *from* the work" – Their cry rose from the midst of the very walls they were forced to build.

The Redal explains further that the Midrash derives the idea that from the verse we mentioned above:

> *I have also seen the pressure* (הלחץ) *with which the Egyptians oppress* (לחצים) *them.*[22]

---

21. Shemos 2:23.
22. Ibid., 3:9.

This "pressure" was the pressure of the bricks which were piled upon them!

We know that Bilam was the one who advised Pharaoh to kill the Jewish sons.[23] It is a marvelous example of "measure for measure" that Bilam is forced to experience the pressure (לחץ) himself that he had caused the Jewish sons! Now we understand why the root לחץ is used in describing the punishment of Bilam in having his leg crushed.[24]

In addition, we can appreciate why the word קיר, "wall," is used. The Jewish sons had been smothered in *walls*![25]

Bilam, himself, is now forced to experience the לחץ of a קיר! Remarkable!

16.3 PILE ON THE PAIN

To fully appreciate the perfection of this punishment, we need to remind ourselves of the covenant made between Yaakov and Lavan.

> *Yaakov took a stone and raised it as a pillar. Yaakov told his brothers [sons]: "Collect stones." They took stones and made a pile. They ate there upon the pile. Lavan called it Yegar Sohadussa, whereas Yaakov called it Gal-ed. Lavan said "This pile should be a witness today between me and you."*[26]

Now let us look at the *Targum Yonason* on the episode of Bilam's leg being crushed:

---

23. See section 7.6. He advised throwing the baby boys into the Nile. Once this happened, it was not long before babies could be smothered in the rows of bricks.
24. The Redal himself adduces the verse of the crushing of Bilam's leg as a support to the idea that לחץ refers to the physical pressure of walls.
25. As mentioned in the *Pirkei D' Rebbe Eliezer* quoted above.
26. Bereishis 31:45-48.

Hashem's angel then stood in a narrow path through the vineyards, the place where Yaakov and Lavan had set up a pile and a pillar on one side and a lookout place on the other and had promised not to cross this boundary with bad intent.[27]

Not only is לבן crushed by אבן, but the stones punishing Lavan are the very stones of the covenant that neither would harm the other! This is another wonderful example of "measure for measure" in the way punishment is meted out by the Almighty – if the covenant is broken, the stones of the covenant will exact retribution. Absolutely perfect![28]

16.4 DEATH BY STONING

Let us examine when stones are used to exact punishment.

The Mishnah lists the four methods of capital punishment in Jewish law.

Four categories of capital punishment are delegated to the court: stoning, burning, the sword and strangulation.[29]

Which offences receive the punishment of stoning?

There are eighteen transgressions:

These are the ones who are stoned: (1) One who cohabits with his mother, (2) with his father's wife, (3) with his daughter-in-law, (4) with a male, (5) with an animal, (6) a woman who brings an animal upon herself, (7) a blasphemer, (8) one who

---

27. *Targum Yonasan* on Bamidbar 22:24. A point which requires further thought is that the description of the making of the covenant implies that the מצפה was not a separately constructed entity. (See Bereishis 31:45-49) The *Targum Yonasan* here clearly understands that the מצפה was a separate entity.

28. What is marvelous is that it was the *Targum Yonasan* who told us that Bilam is really Lavan, as we learned in section 3.1.

29. *Sanhedrin* 7:1 (49b).

serves idols, (9) one who gives of his offspring to Molech, (10) a practitioner of Ov or (11) Yidoni, (12) one who desecrates the Sabbath, (13) one who curses his father or mother, (14) one who cohabits with a betrothed girl, (15) one who entices an individual to idolatry, (16) one who leads astray a city, (17) a sorcerer and (18) a wayward and rebellious son.[30]

If we look at this list carefully, we will see that there is a common denominator. This is a lack of respect for the relationship that is meant to exist between parents and children, and an unwillingness to follow the path of parents.

(1) One who cohabits with his mother – a lack of respect for a mother.

(2) With his father's wife – a lack of respect for a father.

(3) With his daughter-in-law – a lack of respect for the father-son relationship.

(4) With a male – a relationship that cannot produce children.

(5) With an animal – same as (4).

(6) A woman who brings an animal upon herself – same as (4).

(9) One who gives of his offspring to Molech – this involved passing children through fire as a service to the idol Molech. This is total betrayal of the child by the parent.

(13) One who curses his father or mother – a lack of respect toward parents.

(18) A wayward and rebellious son – a lack of respect toward parents.

The above comprises half of the list, and the common thread is evident. Let us examine the others in the list.

(7) A blasphemer – he curses G-d.

(8) One who serves idols.

---

30. Ibid., 7:4 (53a).

(15) One who entices an individual to idolatry.

(16) One who leads astray a city [to idolatry].

The common denominator is a total rejection of the value system of parents!

The idea that idolatry is an abandonment of the path of the parents is expressed clearly by Rashi. In the section of the Torah describing one who entices an individual to idolatry, we read:

> *If your brother, the son of your mother, or your son or your daughter*[31]*... will entice you secretly, saying "Let us go and serve gods of others" – that you did not know, neither you nor your forefathers...* [32]

Rashi comments;

> *"That you did not know, neither you nor your forefathers" – This matter is a great disgrace for you, because even idol worshippers do not discard what has been transmitted to them by their fathers, and this one [the enticer] is telling you "Reject what has been transmitted to you by your fathers."*

Three of the remainder can be considered as one group:

(10) A practitioner of Ov.

(11) A practitioner of Yidoni.

(17) A sorcerer.

Let us start with the first two. What are "Ov" and "Yidoni"?

Rashi explains:

> *"One who consults Ov" – This is a type of supernatural creature called "pisom" which speaks from a person's armpit and can summon up the dead into a person's armpit.*

---

31. Instead of the father leading the child on the path of tradition, the child is enticing the parent to forsake tradition!
32. Devarim 13:7.

> *"And Yidoni" – The person places a bone of an animal called "yedua" into his mouth and the bone speaks through witchcraft.*[33]

What is the connection to relationships with parents?

If a person wants guidance as to what he should do, the appropriate course of action is to consult one's parents and elders. Someone who rejects the path of parents will seek other avenues to obtain direction, even from supernatural forces through witchcraft.

The prohibitions to consult these forces are mentioned several times in the Torah, and it is important to see the context in which they are written.

For example, the first time they are mentioned,

> *Do not turn to the Ovos or Yidonim;*[34] *do not seek to be contaminated through them. I am Hashem your G-d. In the presence of an old person you shall rise and you shall honor the presence of a sage and you shall fear your G-d; I am Hashem.*[35]

An important tool in understanding verses in Torah is to look at the topics which precede or follow them. These are often thematically connected, and can shed light on the section studied.

The very next verse, after the prohibition against turning to Ov or Yidoni, instructs as to appropriate respect for *correct* authority. Turning to Ov and Yidoni is consulting the *wrong* authorities.

The second mention is in the following chapter, immediately after the prohibition to give one's children to Molech. This involved passing the children through fire. This is a total abuse of the position of parents. The next verses say:

> *The person who turns to the Ovos or Yidonim to go astray after*

---

33. Rashi on Devarim 18:11.
34. Plurals of "Ov" and "Yidoni."
35. Vayikra 19:31-32.

> *them, I will concentrate My attention on that person and cut him off from among his people. You shall sanctify yourselves and be holy, for I am Hashem, your G-d. You shall observe My statutes and keep them. I am Hashem, Who sanctifies you. For anyone that curses his father or his mother shall be put to death; he has cursed his father or his mother, his blood is upon him.*[36]

It is amazing! After the prohibition to consult Ov and Yidoni, there is the punishment for cursing father or mother. Both represent a lack of respect for the authority and guidance of parents.

We have already used the tool of examining the etymology of names many times. Let us examine the names Ov and Yidoni and see if they express this idea of rejection of parental authority and guidance.

We have seen[37] that the word for "father," אב, represents a continuation of the *mesorah*, tradition. Without a father, there is not even *aleph-beis*, א–ב. The word "Ov," אוב, is the letters א–ב, with a break in the middle. One who consults Ov is not interested in connection with the *mesorah*.

"Yidoni," ידעוני, is related to the Hebrew meaning "he will make known to me." Instead of looking for guidance from parents, other sources are consulted.

Another transgression that carries the punishment of stoning is sorcery. A sorcerer is using powers from a totally different source than that which his parents have taught him.

It is interesting that the verse which teaches the punishment for sorcery states: מכשפה לא תחיה, which means,

> *Do not let a sorceress live.*[38]

---

36. Ibid., 20:6-9.
37. Section 6:2.
38. Shemos 22:17.

This phrase "do not let live" is only used twice in the Torah.[39] Why is it used here?

The reason that the phrase is used in the context of punishing the practice of witchcraft is that the sorceress is resorting to other authorities to obtain her powers. She should only follow the authority of parents and the path they have taught her. It is fitting that she should not have the gift which her parents gave her – the gift of life. Therefore, "do not let her live."[40]

It is not unexpected to find that Bilam, the arch-exponent of disconnection, uses witchcraft and Yidoni.

We learned[41] that in the battle against Midian, Pinchas took the *tzitz* as a weapon. Rashi explains:

Bilam was together with the Midianites. He used ***witchcraft*** *to enable the kings of Midian to fly and he was flying with them.*[42]

The *tzitz* enabled Pinchas to nullify the witchcraft.

How do we know that Bilam used the forces of Yidoni? The *Ohr Hachayim* asks a fascinating question. The second time Balak tries to take Bilam to curse the Jews we are told:

> *In the morning Balak took Bilam and brought him up to Ba'al Heights from where he could see the edge of the people.*[43]

How could Bilam see any of the Jewish people – they were covered by the Clouds of Glory![44] The *Ohr Hachayim* answers that they

39. The other occurrence is in connection with the nations occupying the land of Israel (Devarim 20:16).
40. The reason for its use in the other occurrence is that the people inhabiting the land were expert in the use of witchcraft. See *Ba'al Haturim*, Devarim 22:17.
41. Section 4.2.
42. Rashi on Bamidbar 31:6.
43. Bamidbar 22:41.
44. See *Ta'anis* 9a. Even though the clouds of glory departed when Aharon died, such that the Canaanites could see the Jews and went to war against them (Rashi on Bamidbar 21:1 and 33:40), Moshe prayed and they returned.

employed supernatural methods, using the bird *"yedua,"*[45] and this enabled them to see part of the nation, but it had no power to reveal the righteous of the nation. Not only did Bilam use witchcraft, he also harnessed the powers of Yidoni. Not surprising![46]

(14) One who cohabits with a betrothed girl. The translation is not absolutely precise. The phrase is actually והבא על נערה המארסה. A נערה *(na'arah)* means a girl who has reached the age of twelve and physical puberty. She is now an adult, fully obliged to keep the commandments. This status lasts for six months, during which time she is still under the jurisdiction of her father. After the six months she is called a בוגרת *(bogeres)*, and is totally independent. As a נערה, even though she is married, her father has rights to her earnings, objects she finds, etc., until she starts living with her husband.

If we look at the verse which teaches the punishment that this girl receives if she is adulterous, we see:

> *They shall take the girl* (הנערה) *to the entrance of* ***her father's house*** *and the people of the city shall pelt her with stones and she shall die, for she had committed a shameful act in Israel, to commit adultery in* ***her father's house****; you shall remove the evil from your midst.*[47]

---

45. The *Ohr Hachayim* interpreted *"yedua"* as a type of bird, as opposed to Rashi who explained that it was an animal. The Rambam, *Hilchos Avodas Kochavim* 6:2, also explains that it is a bird.
46. Moreover, the Ov, Yidoni and other magic, are strongly related to idol-worship customs, and are therefore included in the Rambam's "Laws of Idol Worship" [chapter 11]. As mentioned above, *Sefer Hachinuch* [33] writes that the ultimate aim of honoring parents is the attachment and gratitude to G-d. Being involved with these diverse forms of magic is diametrically opposed to this goal.
47. Devarim 22:21. If the witnesses come before the daughter leaves her father's home, she is stoned at the entrance of the city. (See *Kesubos* 44b-45a) The Ritva explains that, in this case, there is no need for the punishment to be given at the entrance to her father's house, since everyone

Although she is an adult, and is married, she is under her father's jurisdiction. Both she and the adulterer are contravening the jurisdiction that her father is meant to have. Therefore, their punishment is stoning.[48]

(12) One who desecrates the Sabbath. What is the connection between the Sabbath and parents?

We learnt about the command to have awe for parents:

> *Every man, his mother and his father shall you fear and keep My Sabbaths; I am Hashem your G-d.*[49]

Why is the commandment to keep the Sabbath in the same verse as fearing parents? Rashi answers:

> *"And keep my Sabbaths" – The juxtaposition of Sabbath observance with fear of father teaches us that even though I have instructed you about fear of father, if he tells you to desecrate the Sabbath, do not listen to him, and the same applies to all other commandments.*
> *"I am Hashem your G-d" – You and your father are both obliged to honor Me, therefore do not listen to him to nullify My words.*

There is a major difficulty with this explanation. We are not allowed to listen to parents to transgress *any* commandment. If so, why was this idea taught with the Sabbath, one of the strictest and most fundamental commandments? We might think that only for such major commandments must parents be ignored!

The Malbim suggests a masterful explanation.[50] We know that the Almighty created the world in six days and rested on the seventh.

---

knows that she lives there. As such, the entrance to the city is used, where there will be increased publicity.

48. The man also receives the death penalty of stoning. See Devarim 22:23-24.
49. Vayikra 19:3.
50. Commentary on Shemos 20:12.

Resting implies that there was more to create, but that G-d desisted.

What else could have been created? Man, the pinnacle of creation, already existed!

The answer is that G-d would have continued creating people, obviating the need for human parents. Only because He rested on the seventh day is the continuation of the human species through fathers and mothers procreating.

In other words, were it not for the Sabbath, there would be no parents!

Furthermore, the Sabbath is an expression of acknowledgement of G-d as the Creator of the world and our way to express our gratitude to Him for doing so. We repeatedly refer to the Sabbath as "a remembrance of the work of creation." One who has no gratitude to the Creator of the world in which he lives will have no gratitude to those who "created" him.

We have discovered that transgressions which receive stoning have the common theme of lack of respect for the parent-child relationship.

Interestingly, some of the verses that detail these transgressions state explicitly that the punishment is stoning, either by using the verb סקל, or by writing אבן. Seven of them do not mention either. How do we know that these seven also receive stoning?

The answer is that they are derived with a *gezeirah shavah*. We wrote above:[51]

> *A crucial tool for exegetical derivations of Torah laws is the gezeirah shavah. This is the second of the thirteen hermeneutical principles listed by Rebbe Yishmael.*[52]
> *The principle is that if the same, or similar, words are found in two places in the Torah, then we can infer from one place to the*

---

51. Section 8.2.
52. See chapter 8, footnote 13.

other. This is a halachic principle, and is used to derive laws of one section from another. It can be used if there is a tradition from Sinai that the pair of words can be used in such a way.

The verse which teaches the punishment for consulting Ov or Yidoni states:

ואיש או אשה כי יהיה בהם אוב או ידעני מות יומתו באבן ירגמו אתם דמיהם בם:

Any man or woman who is involved with Ov or Yidoni shall be put to death; they shall pelt them with ***stones****, their* ***blood is upon themselves****.*[53]

The Talmud teaches that this verse is the source that reveals that wherever a verse says "their blood is upon themselves," or "his blood is upon him," the connotation is that the punishment is stoning.

In our list of transgressions, it is simply remarkable that *every* verse that does not mention stoning explicitly has one of these phrases.

In other words, if the parent-child relationship is not honored, it is the אבן which exacts punishment. Furthermore, the phrase used to teach seven of the transgressions is "blood upon them/him." This is so appropriate in light of what we have learned about the importance of blood as a symbol of father-son connection.

16.5 ROLLING STONE

We have encountered the concept of *gilgul*, reincarnation.[54]

We have seen that a soul can return as a different person. In fact, a soul can return in a completely different form, not necessarily as a human-being. The evil Bilam, after his death, returns to this world in

53. Vayikra 20:27.
54. Section 3.1.

a *gilgul*. When we read, in *Sha'ar Hagilgulim*, what his *gilgul* is we are dumb-founded:

> *Lavan was reincarnated as Bilam... When Bilam was killed he was reincarnated as a* ***stone.***[55]

Truly amazing!

Bilam, alias Lavan (לא בן), has his chance to atone for his sins as אבן, a stone, the symbol of connection between fathers and sons!

We might think that this is the end of the story, but there is more to come.

---

55. *Sha'ar Hagilgulim*, introduction 22.

17

Naval ideas

17.1 INTRODUCING NAVAL

We have discovered that Bilam was reincarnated as a stone. The Arizal goes further:

Afterwards, Bilam was reincarnated as Naval the Carmelite.[1]

---

1. *Sha'ar Hagilgulim*, introduction 22.
It is appropriate to mention the statement in *Sanhedrin* 105a, "Beor [the father of Bilam] was the same person as Cushan Rishosayim who was the same person as Lavan the Aramean."
The common element of these three is that they are all from Aram. We know that Lavan was from Aram (Bereishis 25:20, 28:2,5). Bilam is referred to as "Bilam son of Beor from Pesor in Aram Naharayim" (Devarim 23:5). The understanding is that Beor was from Aram, not just Bilam. Cushan Rishosayim was a king of Aram who subjugated the Jews after the death of Yehoshua (Shoftim 3:8-9).
How do we reconcile this with what we have learned that Lavan was Bilam, not his father Beor? There are a number of commentaries which explain that "Beor" refers to Bilam, *son of Beor*. (*Eitz Yosef*; *Meloh Haroim*, quoting *Shnei Luchos Habris, Torah Shebichsav, parshas Balak*.)
However, there remains the question of whether Bilam became a stone and then Naval, as taught by the Arizal, or whether he was Cushan Rishosayim. A

The Arizal undoubtedly knew this from divine inspiration. However, if we learn the story of Naval we will find many indications in the text as well. Let us examine I Shmuel chapter 25.[2]

David has already been annointed as king by Shmuel. Shaul pursued David and his followers, trying to kill him.

> [2]*There was a man in Maon whose business was in Carmel. The man was very wealthy; he had three thousand sheep and a thousand goats. He was shearing his sheep in Carmel.* [3]*The man's name was Naval and his wife's name was Avigail; the woman was intelligent and beautiful, but the man was hard-hearted and an evildoer; he was a descendant of Calev.* [4]*David heard in the wilderness that Naval was shearing his sheep.* [5]*David sent ten young men, and David said to the young men, "Go up to Carmel, and go to Naval, and greet him in my name.* [6]*And you shall say, 'Such [success] should be for life! Peace to you and peace to your house and peace to all that is yours.* [7]*And now I have heard that they are shearing for you. Now your shepherds who were with us, we did not shame them and they did not lack anything all the days that they were in Carmel.* [8]*Ask your young men and they will tell you. Therefore let [my] young men find favor in your eyes, for we come at a festive time: please give whatever you can to your servants and to your son, to David.'"*
>
> [9]*David's young men came and spoke in accordance with all these words to Naval in David's name and then they rested.*

---

possible resolution may be based on an idea which we will meet in the coming chapter (section 18.5), that there are many different parts of the soul, and these different parts can return as different *gilgulim*. Thus, the Talmud (*Sanhedrin* 105a) may describe what happened to one part of the soul of Lavan, whereas the Arizal is relating to another part.

2. Since the extracts of text quoted are long and we will be referring back to them, verse numbers have been included here for ease of reference.

> *[10]Naval replied to David's servants and said, "Who is David and who is the son of Yishai? These days there are many servants who are rebellious, each against his master. [11]Should I take my bread and my water and the meat that I have slaughtered for my shearers and give them to men whom I do not know where they come from?"*

David's men return and tell David about Naval's response. He sets out with about four hundred men, intending to kill Naval.

> *[14]One of the young men told Avigail, the wife of Naval, saying, "Behold, David sent messengers from the wilderness to greet our master, but he drove them away. [15]These men were very good to us; we were not shamed nor did we lack anything all the days that we journeyed with them, when we were in the field. [16]They were a wall over us, both by day and by night, all the days we were with them tending the sheep. [17]Now be aware and consider what to do, for evil has been determined against our master and against his entire house, and he is too base a person to speak to."*

On hearing about David's approach, Avigail takes two hundred loaves, two containers of wine, five cooked sheep, five measures of toasted grain, a hundred raisin clusters and two hundred cakes of pressed figs. Without informing her husband, she has them loaded on donkeys and sets out towards David and his men. She gives the provisions to David, who relents from his decision to wipe out Naval and all his male offspring. Avigail returns home.

> *[36]Avigail came to Naval and behold he was having a feast in his house, a feast fit for a king. Naval's heart was pleased with himself and he was very drunk, so she did not tell him anything, minor or major, until the morning light. [37]In the morning, when the effect of the wine had passed, his wife told him of these*

> *matters, his heart died within him and he was as a stone. [38]After about ten days, Hashem smote Naval and he died.*

Did you notice any clues in the story that Naval is a *gilgul* of Lavan/Bilam?

17.2 FORWARDS AND BACKWARDS

An idea which can provide insight into personalities which we encounter in Torah is that names which share the same letters may indicate a connection between the people who have those names.

If we look at the name לבן, we will see that the letters are the same as those of Naval, **נבל**.[3]

Another tool in Torah-interpretation is that of acronyms – often a word is interpreted as an acronym of various names or ideas.

לבן is an acronym for three *gilgulim* he will be as people: לבן, **בלעם** and **נבל**. Since Naval is the last of the three, his name is an acronym for the three *gilgulim* he has been as people, looking back in time: **נבל**, **בלעם** and לבן.[4]

17.3 MY GRANDFATHER THE SPY

In verse 3, we read that Naval "was a descendant of Calev." Who was Calev?

Calev was one of the twelve spies sent by Moshe to spy out the land of Canaan.[5] During their mission,

> ויעלו בנגב ויבא עד חברון...
>
> *They ascended in the Negev and he came to Hebron...*[6]

---

3. Arizal, *Sha'ar Hagilgulim*, introduction 36.
4. Ibid.
5. Bamidbar 13:6.
6. Ibid., v. 22.

There seems to be a contradiction: we are told "they ascended" in the plural, and then "he came," in the singular!

Rashi resolves the problem:

> *"He came to Hebron" – Calev went by himself. He prayed by the graves of the fathers that he should not be swayed to join his colleagues in their scheme. That is why it says, "I will give him the land which he has trodden on"*[7] *and it is written, "And they gave Hebron to Calev."*[8]

What saves Calev from falling prey to the evil designs of the spies? Connection to fathers. He goes to pray at the cave of Machpelah. In that merit, he acquires the city of Hebron, which contains the burial place of the fathers.

Bilam is reincarnated as Naval, a man descended from Calev who *is* connected to fathers. The example of his ancestor should give him considerable help in repairing the damage caused in previous *gilgulim*. Will Naval succeed?

17.4 FASCINATING SHEAR

We have seen that, if a word rarely occurs in the Torah, the occurrences are often thematically connected.

In verse 4, we read:

> וישמע דוד במדבר כי גזז נבל את צאנו:
>
> *David heard in the wilderness that Naval was shearing his sheep.*

---

7. Devarim 1:36.
8. Shoftim 1:20.

There are only two[9] men in the entire Tenach, mentioned by name, who shear (גזז) sheep. One is Naval. Who is the other?

ולבן הלך לגזז את צאנו ותגנב רחל את התרפים אשר לאביה:

Lavan had gone to shear his sheep, and Rachel stole the idols belonging to her father.[10]

Amazing. The only two people who do this activity just happen to have the same name (letters rearranged) and, in fact, just happen to be the same person!

What is גוזז, shearing? It is one of the thirty-nine activities forbidden on the Sabbath, and is defined as disconnecting something from its place of growth.[11]

In other words, Lavan and Naval are the only two examples who perform this activity – disconnecting from living creatures. Disconnection is the essence of Lavan (לא בן) and we find it again with Naval.

Just as Lavan did his utmost to prevent Yaakov having any sheep, in spite of his hard work for Lavan, so too Naval refuses to give David any sheep, even though his flocks benefitted from David's protection.

We read in verse 16 that one of Naval's young men testifies about the protection Naval's sheep received from David and his men:

They were a wall over us, both by day and by night, all the days we were with them tending the sheep.

The protection was both "by day and by night."

Yaakov tells Lavan how he cared for Lavan's sheep:

---

9. The one other person mentioned by name who shears sheep is Yehudah: "And Tamar was informed saying, 'Behold your father-in-law is going up to Timnah to shear (לגז) his sheep.'" (Bereishis 38:13) However, the verb used there is a different form – לגז rather than לגזז. The only times we find לגזז are with Lavan and Naval.
10. Bereishis 31:19.
11. That is also the definition of קוצר, harvesting. The difference is that קוצר relates to plants, whereas גוזז applies to animals.

"By day scorching heat consumed me and frost by night; sleep left my eyes."[12]

The parallel is perfect. Once again, the protection is twenty-four hours a day and is repaid with absolute ingratitude. We have seen the *Sefer Hachinuch* who writes that the basis of connection with parents is to foster the attribute of gratitude. Lavan and Naval have no gratitude at all.

17.5 "SON OF YISHAI"

In verse 10, we read Naval's response on being asked to give David some of his wealth:

Naval replied to David's servants and said, "Who is David and who is the son of Yishai? These days there are many servants who are rebellious, each against his master."

Not only does he refer to David in a contemptuous manner but he says "and who is the son of Yishai?" The relationship with father is held in total disdain. This misuse of the power of speech is something which we have seen with both Lavan and Bilam.

17.6 BASE בל

We have seen that Naval is the *gilgul* of Lavan. Since Lavan and Bilam share the same essence we should expect Naval to have connections to Bilam. Are there any textual clues that this is so?

When one of Naval's young men warns Avigail of the impending danger, he says:

12. Bereishis 31:40.

> *"Now be aware and consider what to do, for evil has been determined against our master and against his entire house, and he is too base (בן בליעל) a person to speak to."*[13]

Similarly, Avigail, when speaking to David, says,

> *"Please, let not my master set his heart against this base man (איש הבליעל)."*[14]

Twice Naval is referred to as בליעל.

The Arizal reveals that these are allusions to the fact that Naval is a *gilgul* of Bilam.

We have encountered the tool of *gematria* and know that if two ideas share the same numerical value this can indicate a thematic connection.[15]

The *gematria* of בליעל is 142, the same as that of בלעם.[16]

The Arizal teaches us, in a number of places in his writings, that Hevel (הבל), the son of Adam, had a good part to his soul and an evil part. The good part of Hevel is represented by the letter *hei* (ה) which is reincarnated in Moshe (משה) and the bad part is represented by the letters *beis-lamed* (בל) which is reincarnated in לבן, בלעם and נבל. Similarly, we find the letters *beis-lamed* (בל) in the word בליעל.[17]

We have seen that one of the *gilgulim* of Lavan was a stone, אבן. Here, we do not see the letter *lamed* (ל), only *beis* (ב). Why do we not find both letters of בל? One might think that the answer is that these letters only appear in the names of people and not inanimate objects. The real answer is amazing, as we will see shortly.

---

13. I Shmuel 25:17.
14. Ibid., v. 25.
15. See sections 5.1, 10.14, 13.2.
16. *Sefer Halikutim*, I Shmuel ch. 25; *Likutei Torah*, I Shmuel ch.25.
17. It is interesting to note that also the name בבל contains the letters בל, in light of what we saw in chapter 8, sections 1-3.

17.7 "MY FATHER, THE PILE"

When Avigail (אביגיל) meets David, she greets him and, after taking the blame for not responding to his request for food, he responds:

> *David said to Avigal* (אביגל), *"Blessed be Hashem, G-d of Israel, who sent you today to meet me."*[18]

Here, she is not referred to as אביגיל, but as אביגל, without the second *yud* (י). Why? The kabbalistic works teach us that she was a reincarnation of Leah, daughter of Lavan.[19]

The word אביגל is a combination of two words: אבי which means "my father," and גל which means "a pile." This refers to the father of Leah who made a covenant with Yaakov with a pile of stones.[20]

Naval, alias Lavan, has a reminder, in the form of his wife, of his obligation towards Yaakov and his descendants.

What clues are there that אביגל refers to Leah and not Rachel, also a daughter of Lavan?

There is a clear parallel in the actions of Leah, her daughter Dinah, and Avigail that indicate a strong connection.

Avigail goes out to David, initiates conversation with him, and the last words she tells him are:

> *"When Hashem will do good to my master [i.e., David], you should remember your maidservant."*[21]

Chazal teach us that she was intimating to David that when her husband would die, she would want to be wife to David and that he should remember her.[22] Indeed, this is what happens. The verse after

---

18. I Shmuel 25:32.
19. Arizal, *Sha'ar Hagilgulim*, introduction 36. See *Be'er Moshe* on I Shmuel ch. 25.
20. See sections 2.6 and 7.3.
21. I Shmuel 25:31.
22. *Megillah* 14b, *Bava Kama* 92b.

the death of Naval tells us that when David heard of the death of Naval, he took Avigail as a wife.

Turning to Leah, we know that Rachel agreed that Yaakov should be with Leah on a night that he was meant to be with Rachel, in return for the mandrakes which Reuven had found.[23]

> *When Yaakov came home from the field that evening, Leah went out to meet him. She said, "You will come to me, for I have hired you with my son's mandrakes."*[24]

Leah goes out to her husband and initiates the relationship.

Leah's daughter is Dinah, about whom we read:

> *Dinah, the daughter of Leah whom she had borne to Yaakov, went out to see the daughters of the land.*[25]

Why is Dinah referred to here as the daughter of her mother – normally the father's name is used!

Rashi answers the question:

> *"The daughter of Leah" – She was not the daughter of Yaakov?*[26] *It is because of her going out that she is called "the daughter of Leah," because she also was one who went out, as it says, "Leah went out to meet him."*

Leah goes out to her husband. Her daughter, Dinah, goes out as well – inheriting this attribute.

Avigail goes out and, in essence, proposes to David.

That is our clue that "Avigal" is the *gilgul* of Leah and not of Rachel. It is Leah, not Rachel, who goes out to her husband, as Avigail goes out to David.

---

23. Bereishis 30:14-15.
24. Ibid., v. 16.
25. Ibid., 34:1.
26. I.e., why is she called the daughter of Leah?

Avigail tries to repair the damage caused by Lavan/Bilam/Naval. Unlike Lavan and Naval, who want to give nothing, she gives generously. Unlike all three, who curse and speak with harmful intentions, she blesses David effusively, both with regard to this world and the next.[27] Unlike Bilam, who rides a donkey to go and curse, she rides a donkey to go and bless.

However, Naval himself has failed miserably. What happens to him?

17.8 STONE DRUNK

When Avigail returns home, Naval is feasting and is inebriated. She waits until the morning:

> *In the morning, when the effect of the wine had passed, his wife told him of these matters, his heart died within him and he became as a stone* (והוא היה לאבן).[28]

The Arizal reveals:

> *When Bilam was killed he was reincarnated as a stone, which is an inert object (literally: "silent"), to atone for the incantations he uttered with his mouth.*
>
> *Subsequently, he was reincarnated as Naval the Carmelite, a first return to this world to make amends. When he verbally disgraced David saying, "Who is David and who is the son of Yishai?" David wanted to kill him, since the reason he was alive was only to make amends for the evil speech of Bilam. Not only had he not made amends, but he had added iniquity, by once again sinning with his speech, cursing David the king of Israel.*
>
> *Naval became aware that he had formerly been reincarnated as a stone to amend the evil speech of Bilam, and instead he*

---

27. See *Shabbos* 152b.
28. I Shmuel 25:37.

had returned to his evil ways. That is why "his heart died within him," remembering that he had formerly been a stone. Therefore it does not say "and he became a stone" (ויהי לאבן), *but "and he was as a stone"* (והוא היה לאבן), *implying that he had already been a stone.*[29]

This shows us that it is very important to examine the tenses of verbs used. If the tense employed is different than what we would expect, the reason should be investigated.

The use of the past tense indicates that Naval had previously been a stone. If we look at the phrase closely, what we find is remarkable.

The word לאבן is לא בן. The very same problem we found with Lavan still exists.[30] No improvement has occurred.

We noted above that in all the *gilgulim* of Lavan there are the letters *beis* (ב) and *lamed* (ל) from the name הבל – לבן, בלעם and נבל. This prompted us to ask why this is not so with the reincarnation as a stone – אבן.

The word that tells us about the *gilgul* as a stone is לאבן. There we *do* find the letters *beis* (ב) and *lamed* (ל)! Furthermore, the word לאבן contains the first letters of all of the *gilgulim* – לבן, אבן, בלעם and נבל.[31] Amazing!

Is there no hope for any improvement? Has Naval failed for eternity?

We need to examine one more *gilgul*.

---

29. *Sha'ar Hagilgulim*, introduction 22. See also introduction 29.
30. See section 7.1.
31. See *Ben Yehoyoda, Rosh Hashanah* 18a. The letter *beis* also alludes to the final *gilgul*, which will be introduced in chapter 18!

18

Barzilai from Gilad

18.1 WHO IS BARZILAI?

Naval receives another chance to make amends.

The Arizal revealed to us that Naval returns in a subsequent *gilgul* as Barzilai the Giladite.[1] Who was Barzilai, and what clues are there that this was so? Does he succeed this time around?

Let us learn about Barzilai.

When King David's son Avshalom attempts to usurp the throne, David and his followers are forced to flee.

> *When David came to Machanayim, Shovi the son of Nachash from Rabbah of the children of Ammon, Machir son of Amiel from Lo-devar and* ***Barzilai of Gilad*** *from Rogelim, brought bedding, bowls, pottery, wheat, barley, flour, toasted grain, beans, lentils, toasted legumes, honey, butter,* ***sheep****, and cow's milk cheeses, for David and the people who were with him to eat, for they said, "The people are hungry, weary, and thirsty in the wilderness."*[2]

---

1. *Sha'ar Hagilgulim*, introduction 36, *Sha'ar Hapesukim, parshas Balak.*
2. II Shmuel 17:27-29.

Lavan did not want Yaakov to have anything and did his utmost to prevent Yaakov earning any sheep.[3]

Naval refused to give David any of his huge flock of three thousand sheep and one thousand goats.[4]

Barzilai, though, gives David with utmost generosity, and his gift includes sheep.

18.2 IRON-MAN

We know that a person's name has great significance and is an important tool in understanding his essence.

Let us look at the name ברזלי. Firstly, the name contains the letters *beis* (ב) and *lamed* (ל) which we have learned are a part of each *gilgul* of Lavan.[5]

The first two letters are *beis-reish* (בר), which means "son" in Aramaic.[6]

It is wonderful to see that Lavan, the Aramean who speaks Aramaic,[7] has finally become a son. Furthermore, as we will see, Barzilai is a man very much connected to parents and children.

We learned[8] about Lavan's intentions towards his son-in-law, daughters and grandchildren – he would have harmed them all if G-d would not have appeared to him and warned him to refrain from even speaking badly to Yaakov.

How many daughters did Lavan have?

When Lavan catches up with Yaakov, he warns Yaakov:

> *"If you will ill-treat my daughters or if you will marry wives in*

---

3. See section 7.13.
4. I Shmuel 25:11, quoted in section 17.1.
5. Section 17.6.
6. See section 10.14.
7. See section 2.6.
8. Section 7.10.

addition to my daughters... G-d is a witness between me and you."[9]

Why is the phrase "my daughters" used twice – surely "them" would have sufficed in place of the second usage!

Apparently unnecessary repetitions are not really unnecessary and teach important ideas.

Rashi comments:

"My daughters... my daughters" – [The word "daughters" is written] twice, since Bilhah and Zilpah were also his daughters, born from a concubine.[10]

So, *all* of Yaakov's wives are daughters of Lavan.

We have seen that a tool used in Torah interpretation is the realization that words or phrases can be an acronym for a number of related words.[11]

The Arizal reveals in a number of places that the acronym for the four wives of Yaakov (בלהה רחל זלפה לאה) is ברזל, which means "iron."[12]

---

9. Bereishis 31:50.
10. See section 11.1.
11. See sections 17.2 and 17.8.
12. See, for example, *Sefer Eitz Chayim*, gate 49, ch. 9.
    Knowing this, we can really appreciate one of the teachings of the Arizal (*Sefer Eitz Ha'daas Tov, parshas Eikev*): The Torah describes the land of Israel as, ארץ אשר אבניה ברזל ומהרריה תחצב נחשת - a land whose stones are iron and from whose mountains you will mine copper. (Devarim 8:9)
    The verse is replete with allusions to our fathers and mothers. The Arizal points out that we see the word ברזל, an allusion to the mothers of the twelve tribes.
    A tool sometimes encountered in Torah-interpretation is that of acrostics, in which the first or last letters of a series of words spell out an encrypted message.
    For a thorough treatment of many examples of acrostic, the reader is encouraged to obtain the fascinating work *Niflaos Mi'Torosechah*, by R. Mordechai Aranovski.

Lavan wanted to harm his four daughters and their husband. The first letters of the names of the four daughters and their husband Yaakov spell the word ב.ר.ז.ל.י., the *gilgul* of Lavan.

This time around, though, as Barzilai, he wants to help their descendants, David and his followers.

Barzilai is called בַּרְזִלַּי הַגִּלְעָדִי, of an area called Gilad. The name Gilad has exactly the same spelling as גַּלְעֵד, the name given to the pile of covenant between Yaakov and Lavan.[13] Now he has become someone who remembers and abides by the covenant.

He lives in a town called רֹגְלִים *(Rogelim)*. We do not find this town mentioned anywhere in Tenach other than in connection with Barzilai.[14]

If the name of a place is mentioned which we do not find anywhere else, this indicates that the name is to be interpreted as revealing a deeper connected idea.[15]

This place name is written without a *vav* (ו), and can be read as רַגְלַיִם, meaning "legs." We saw[16] that the leg represents the son continuing the father's path, and that Bilam's leg is crushed. Barzilai has both legs! He is connected to both parents and children, as we will see.

The Arizal reveals that the first letters of the words אבניה ברזל ומהרריה תחצב spell אבות, the word for "fathers."

We have seen, in section 3.4, that mountains are a symbol for fathers. (See also Yeshayahu 52:1-2, where Avraham and Sarah, our ancestors, are compared to rocks.)

Therefore, this is a land which has "stones."

The land of Israel is ours because the Almighty promised it to our fathers.

13. Bereishis 31:47,48.
14. II Shmuel 17:27, 19:32.
15. See Rashi, Devarim 1:1 ; Maharal, *Nesivos Olam*, *Nesiv Ha'anavah* ch.7.
16. Section 16.1

18.3 HOW MANY VERY GREAT MEN WERE THERE?

After Avshalom is killed and the rebellion against David is quashed,

> ***Barzilai***[17] *of Gilad came down from Rogelim, and he crossed the Yarden with the king to send him off from the Yarden.* ***Barzilai*** *was very old, eighty years of age. He had provided for the king when he dwelt in Machanayim, for he was a very wealthy man. The king said to* ***Barzilai****, "Cross over with me and I shall provide for you with me in Yerushalayim."*
> ***Barzilai*** *said to the king, "How long have I to live that I should go up with the king to Yerushalayim? I am eighty years old today. Can I discern between good and bad? Can your servant taste what I eat or drink? Can I hear the voice of male or female singers? Why should your servant be a burden any more to my master the king? I will accompany the king across the Yarden for a bit, but why should the king recompense me with this reward? Please let your servant return, that I may die in my own city, by the grave of my father and my mother. Behold, your servant Chimham will cross over with my lord the king. Do for him that which is good in your eyes."*
> *The king said, "Chimham will cross over with me and I shall do for him that which is good in your eyes. Anything you choose for me I shall do for you."*
> *All the people then crossed over the Yarden and the king crossed over. The king kissed* ***Barzilai*** *and blessed him, and he returned to his place.*[18]

Let us find the clues that indicate who Barzilai was.

---

17. The reason for the use of a bold font for the name "Barzilai" each of the five times it occurs in this section will be explained in section 18.4, footnote 23.
18. II Shmuel 19:32-40.

We are told "he was a very wealthy man." The Hebrew is: איש גדול הוא מאד, literally "a very great man."

Where else do we find a man described similarly?

The first time we meet Naval, we are told,

> *There was a man in Maon whose business was in Carmel.* ***The man was very wealthy****; he had three thousand sheep and a thousand goats.*[19]

The Hebrew is והאיש גדול מאד – these are exactly the same words that are used to describe Barzilai.

We have seen the tool of aggadic *gezeirah shavah* – that if the same, or similar, words are found in two places in the Torah, then we can infer ideas from one place to the other. This is especially significant if the word or phrase occurs rarely.[20]

Naval and Barzilai are the only people in the whole of Tenach described as being "a very great man."[21] The connection between them is clear.

Are there any clues that Barzilai is also a *gilgul* of Lavan and Bilam?

---

19. I Shmuel 25:2. See section 17.1.
20. See section 8.2; section 16.1, fn. 14; sections 16.4 and 17.4.
21. We do find a similar phrase regarding Moshe: "Also *the man Moshe was very great* in the land of Egypt, in the eyes of the servants of Pharaoh and in the eyes of the people." (Shemos 11:3) The Hebrew is **גם האיש משה גדול מאד בארץ מצרים בעיני עבדי פרעה ובעיני העם**.
    Here though, the word גדול is not juxtaposed with the word איש, but with משה.
    In fact, there is only one other occurrence of the phrase איש גדול, and that relates to Naaman (II Melachim 5:1). There, though, there is no mention of מאד.
    The only two instances of איש גדול together with מאד are Naval and Barzilai.
    Why, when describing Barzilai, is the word הוא added - איש גדול **הוא** מאד? R. Shmuel Vital, in a note to *Sha'ar Hapesukim, parshas Balak*, explains that this alludes to the fact that he is the very same soul as the other person described as והאיש גדול מאד.

18.4 FINALLY CONNECTED TO PARENTS

When David offers Barzilai to come with him to Yerushalayim, he refuses, giving the reason,

> *"Please let your servant return, that I may die in my own city, by the grave of my father and my mother."*[22]

He is now a man connected to parents.[23]

When David tries to repay the kindness he had received, Barzilai refuses and says,

> *"Behold, your servant Chimham will cross over with my lord the king. Do for him that which is good in your eyes."*[24]

Who was Chimham? Rashi clarifies:

> *"Your servant Chimham" – He was his son.*

Not only does Barzilai have a close relationship with David, but Barzilai's son will continue in the path of his father, staying together with David in Yerushalayim.

It is fascinating to read what David instructs his son Shlomo, shortly before his death:

> *"Do kindness with the sons of Barzilai; let them eat at your*

---

22. II Shmuel 19:38.
23. In fact, he now fulfills the entire Torah. We learn in the Midrash: Rabbi Yehudah taught, "The name 'Barzilai' is written five times in the section [II Shmuel 19:32-40], corresponding to the five books of Moshe. [See the section quoted in full in section 18:3, with the five occurrences indicated by a bold font.] This teaches us that anyone who feeds a portion to a righteous man, it is considered as if he has fulfilled the five books of the Torah." (*Bereishis Rabbah* 58:8; *Yalkut Shimoni, Bereishis* ch. 23, *remez* 102; ibid., I Melachim ch. 2, *remez* 170.)
    When Barzilai provides for David, it is as though he kept the entire Torah. He has fully rectified the actions of his predecessors – Lavan, Bilam and Naval.
24. II Shmuel 19:38.

table because they provided for me when I fled from your brother Avshalom."[25]

The relationship between David and Barzilai will have continuity to the next generation, with Shlomo showing kindness to Chimham[26] and his brothers.

18.5 RETURNING TO HIS PLACE

The last mention of Barzilai himself is when he leaves David:

וישק המלך לברזלי ויברכהו **וישב למקמו:**

*The king kissed Barzilai and blessed him, and **he returned to his place.***[27]

Where else do we find someone who "returned to his place"? The last time we meet Lavan we read:

וישכם לבן בבקר וינשק לבניו ולבנותיו ויברך אתהם וילך **וישב לבן למקמו:**

*Lavan awoke early in the morning; he kissed his sons and his daughters and blessed them; Lavan went and **returned to his place.***[28]

---

25. I Melachim 2:7.
26. The name Chimham (כִּמְהָם) is also significant. It is spelled like the word כְּמוֹהֶם, meaning *"like them."* (See, for example, Shoftim 8:18.)
The Arizal explains that it is similar to a word uttered by Bilam:
מי מנה עפר יעקב ומספר את רבע ישראל תמת נפשי מות ישרים ותהי אחריתי כמהו:
"Who can count the dust of Yaakov and number the seed of Yisrael? Let my soul die the death of the just and let my end be *like his.*" (Bamidbar 23:10)
Bilam prays to have a good end. He does not want to live like Yisrael, with the obligations of the Torah, but he wants to die like him, with eternal bliss.
When does Bilam finally become "like them," כמוהם, being one with Yisrael? It is fulfilled with Chimham, כמהם, the son of his *gilgul* Barzilai, staying close to David and being one of those who eats with him and, in turn, with David's son Shlomo.
27. II Shmuel 19:40.

When Bilam leaves, having failed to curse the Jewish people, we read:

> ויקם בלעם וילך **וישב למקמו** וגם בלק הלך לדרכו:
>
> *Bilam arose and went and **returned to his place**. Balak also went on his way.*[29]

The *only* three times we find a man who "returned to his place" are Lavan, Bilam and Barzilai! This is not surprising, since they are, in essence, the same person!

A number of interesting questions arise from what we have learned:

1. What is the deeper significance of "returning to one's place"?
2. We have seen that Lavan returned as a stone and as Naval. Why do the stone and Naval not "return to their place"?
3. How is it possible that Naval and Barzilai were both *gilgulim* of Bilam – they lived at the same time![30]

The concept of "returning to one's place" connotes the soul leaving this physical world and returning to the spiritual dimension.

If the soul achieved all that it needed to, it does not need any further *gilgul*; if the soul was not successful, it may return in another *gilgul*. When there is a *gilgul* as an inanimate object, where there is no free will, the phrase "returning to one's place" will not be used.

A soul can return as part of a person living at the same time. This can be understood in light of the fact that there are different parts of

---

28. Bereishis 32:1.
29. Bamidbar 24:25.
30. We read that Barzilai said to David that he was eighty years old. (II Shmuel 19:36) We know that David lived to the age of seventy. This can be derived from the fact he was thirty years old when he became king and he reigned for forty years (II Shmuel 5:4). If so, Naval, who had refused to feed David before David parts from Barzilai, must have lived at the same time as Barzilai.

the soul. The *Sefer Hagilgulim*[31] teaches us that every soul is comprised of 613 sparks. Part of a soul can leave one person and enter another, even if both are alive.[32]

For example, the Arizal revealed that the soul of Yisro returned as part of Korach, even though Yisro and Korach lived at the same time.[33] Similarly, the soul of Naval became part of Barzilai. Since the soul of Naval became part of someone already living, it was not necessary that it "returned to its place."

We have finally arrived at our destination:

- Barzilai succeeds in his assignment.
- He is connected to his parents.
- He generously provides for the descendants of Yaakov.
- His son follows in his path.
- He returns to his place, having fulfilled his task.
- We do not read again that anyone "returned to his place," because there was no further fixing that was required.[34]

Mission accomplished!

---

31. Ch.4.
32. Strictly speaking, this is not called a *gilgul*. The Arizal taught that when a soul enters someone other than at birth, it is called *"ibur,"* עיבור, rather than *"gilgul,"* גלגול. See *Sha'ar Hagilgulim*, introduction 2.
33. *Sha'ar Hapesukim, parshas Balak.*
34. See, however, *Sha'ar Hagilgulim*, introduction 36, where the Arizal lists other *gilgulim* after Barzilai. Although Barzilai "fixed" what he needed to, there were other aspects of Hevel that were still imperfect, and the subsequent *gilgulim* were required to perfect those aspects.

Appendix I

Tools of Torah investigation

The following is a list of tools used in this book with references to sections where they have been used.

Acrostic

Often the first or last letters of a series of words spell out an encrypted message.

Section 18.2, fn.12.

Acronym

Often a word is interpreted as an acronym of various names or ideas.

Sections 17.2, 17.8, 18.2.

Aggadic *gezeirah shavah*

If the same, or similar, words are found in two places in the Torah, then we can infer ideas from one place to the other. This is especially significant if the word or phrase occurs rarely.

Sections 8.2, 16.4, 17.4, 18.3, 18.5.

Analogy

Often a *mashal*, analogy will be used to explain an idea. The *nimshal*, underlying lesson, needs to be fathomed.

Section 15.6.

Definite article

The use of the definite article implies we have encountered this object earlier.

Section 3.9.

Divine names

Sometimes, a name that appears to be a name of G-d, and as such should be holy, in fact has no sanctity, since it actually refers to idols.

Section 2.5.

Doubling of a name

The doubling of a name indicates that the person has a portion in the World to Come.

Section 11.3.

Etymological connections

The etymological connections between a word used and similar words should be examined.

Section 3.8, fn. 36; section 5.2, fn. 15; sections 10.4, 10.5, 10.9, 10.14, 11.1, 12.4, 13.5, 14.2, 14.3, 16.1.

Euphemisms

Sometimes certain words or phrases are not meant to be interpreted literally, but as euphemisms.

Sections 5.2, 5.3, 7.8.

Final *nun*

The addition of the final *nun* (ן), often indicates a continuous involvement with the activity described.

Section 6.3.

First mention of a word or concept

The first mention of a word or concept is the archetypal example of that word or idea.

Section 3.3, fn. 23.

Gematria

The numerical value of a word or phrase can shed light on the concept discussed.

Sections 5.1, 10.14, 13.2, 17.6.

Gilgulim

If kabbalistic sources reveal that one person in Tenach is a *gilgul* of another, the personality of one may shed light on the other.

Sections 3.1-3.11, 16.5, 17.1, 17.3, 17.6, 17.7, 17.8, 18.1, 18.5.

Interchangeable letters

Certain phonetically connected letters are often interchangeable. The different etymological connections between the different readings should be examined.

Section 10.14.

Interruption of connected subjects

If two apparently connected subjects are interrupted by an apparently unconnected subject, the reason should be investigated.

Sections 10.3, 10.10.

Letters – their symbolism

Individual letters have their own meaning, symbolism and significance.

Sections 6.3, 13.2, 17.6.

Measure for measure

Divine punishment is exacted in a form of "measure for measure," matching the nature of the transgression. Similarly, divine reward matches the nature of the meritorious deed performed.

Sections 4.5, 7.6, 7.12, 7.13, 10.7, 10.12, 13.4, 16.3.

Missing characters

If one of the characters in a story is suddenly absent, or his name is absent, the reason should be investigated.

Section 2.2, fn. 8; section 2.3; section 2.4.

Missing letters

Sometimes words or names are spelled without one of their letters. The reason should be investigated.

Sections 3.3, 18.2.

Motifs and recurring themes

If there are motifs or recurring themes, these will often shed light on the depth of the section in which they occur.

Sections 1.6, 1.7.

Multiple explanations in Rashi

If Rashi writes more than one explanation to a word or phrase, the different explanations are often complementary, rather than conflicting with each other.

Section 12.3.

Multiple meanings of the same word or phrase

If a word or phrase has multiple meanings, all the options should be examined to see if they are possible explanations.

Section 1.4, fn. 12; section 3.6; section 5.2, fn. 12 and 13; section 5.3; section 7.8, fn. 52; section 8.1; section 9.3; section 10.4; section 12.3.

Multiple occurrences of an event

If an event occurs several times, the significance should be investigated.

Section 3.8.

Names – their significance in Torah

The name of a person or object describes the essence of that person or object.

Sections 1.2, 1.5, 3.1, 4.3; section 6.5, fn. 12; section 8.1; sections 11.1, 11.2, 15.3, 17.2, 17.6, 17.7, 18.4.

Names which share the same letters

Names which share the same letters may indicate a connection between the people who have those names.

Section 17.2.

Number of occurrences of a word or name in a section

The number of times a word or name occurs in a section is often significant.

Section 6.5, fn. 10; section 18.4.

Paragraph breaks

The use of, or the absence of, paragraph breaks is highly significant.

Section 3.10.

Parshah names

An idea which can give insights into portions of the Torah is that the *name* of the weekly *parshah (Torah-reading)* often has significance and can shed light on that which occurs in that *parshah.*

Section 12.7.

Place names

If a place is mentioned by name, the significance should be examined.

Sections 3.2, 8.3; section 17.1, fn.1; section 18.2.

Preceding and following sections

Looking at the preceding and following sections in the Torah often sheds light on the section studied.

Section 16.4.

Prefixes and suffixes

Seemingly unnecessary or grammatically incorrect prefixes and suffixes should be examined.

Section 3.3.

P'sik

The use of a *p'sik,* a cantillation symbol indicating a break, indicates some form of thematic break.

Section 11.3, fn. 22.

Repetition of words

Apparently unnecessary repetitions are not really unnecessary and teach ideas.

Section 4.2, fn. 12; section 18.2.

Singular/plural forms

The use, in verbs and nouns, of singular where plural might be expected, or vice versa, is highly significant.

Section 1.2, fn. 8; section 1.7, fn. 27; section 2.1; section 7.10; sections 10.3, 10.7; section 11.3, fn. 18; section 17.3.

Spacing between words

Occasionally, the spaces between words in a section of a Torah scroll are of unusual length. This is sometimes so in Nach as well. This gives the section a distinctive appearance. The reason for the unusual spacing should be investigated.

Section 8.4.

Superfluous words or phrases

Apparently superfluous words or phrases are not superfluous, but to teach an idea.

Section 5.3, fn. 24; section 7.6; section 14.2, fn. 16.

Synonyms

There is no such thing as a perfect synonym in the Torah. The shades of meaning that differentiate between the similar words must be understood.

Section 10.14.

Tense

If the tense used seems to be incorrect, the reason should be investigated.

Section 17.8.

Two-letter roots

Hebrew words are based on three-letter roots. R. Samson Raphael Hirsch and others demonstrate that three-letter roots which start with the same two letters are thematically connected. In other words, there is a concept of a two-letter root.

Section 10.14.

Word contractions

Sometimes one word is to be understood as a contraction of two or more words or ideas.

Sections 6.1, 6.2, 7.1, 8.1, 11.2, 15.3, 15.4, 16.4, 17.7, 17.8.

Words in languages other than Hebrew

When languages other than Hebrew are used, the reason should be examined.

Section 2.6.

Words used that are not the normal words for the idea

If a word is used which is not the normal word for the idea, the reason should be investigated.

Section 16.1.

Word order

If the order of words seems strange, the reason should be investigated.

Section 11.3.

Appendix II

What can we do to make Chumash study a WOW?

Chumash study has often been ignored or sidelined. This happens for two reasons: first, it is too simple and second, it is too difficult.

It is too simple because we are taught the stories of Chumash in kindergarten and school, so we associate them with childhood. This results in the mistaken belief that Chumash is not a subject for "mature" study, in contrast to Talmud.

It is too difficult because when you study Chumash as an adult, you find that the language can be ambiguous, allusive and strange. The stories of Chumash, which are greatly simplified for children, contain subtleties, subtexts and moral dilemmas that challenge any serious student.

Chumash is one of the most exciting areas of Torah study. It is accessible: much of the text has a surface simplicity which allows students to gain a basic mastery quickly. At the same time, deeper study offers the excitement of exploration, discovery and personal insights.

In writing this book, I hope to encourage teachers and students to revisit Chumash and enjoy the thrill of learning the most important book ever written.

In this appendix, I have tried to suggest some ways that this thrill can be achieved. The ideas that follow are by no means an exhaustive list of suggestions, but are intended to prompt thought and discussion of what we can, and should, be doing to inspire excitement in the study of Chumash.

Come without preconceptions

We should teach Chumash and Nach to all students, of whatever age, in a way which assumes no previous exposure to the stories and no preconceptions.

For example, one of the most famous stories in Chumash is that of Noah and the ark. Those that remember the story "know" that Noah brought into the ark two of every type of animal and seven of the "kosher" animals. It is a fascinating educational experience to learn the commentary of the Malbim and see that not everything is necessarily as we thought. The Malbim's forensic examination of the text makes you question your assumptions about how many of each species were actually brought into the ark.[1]

Appreciate the different approaches

We should be giving our students the tools to plumb the depths of Torah.

Firstly, they should be introduced to the idea that there are multiple layers of meaning in every section of Torah. It should be standard knowledge that there are four primary areas of

1. See Malbim on Bereishis 6:13 – 7:9.

interpretation, referred to by the acronym פרדס.[2] This stands for the initial letters of:

i) פשט *(pshat)* – the straightforward understanding of the text.

ii) רמז *(remez)* – allusions in the text to people, ideas and concepts which are not apparent from a straightforward reading of the text.

iii) דרש *(drash)* – a non-literal interpretation flowing from some apparent problem with the text, such as an unnecessary word or letter, an unusual word order, or a grammatical inconsistency.

There are a number of key principles used in this area and the workings of these should be clearly understood. For example, the thirteen principles of Rebbe Yishmael, which we say in morning prayers, should be part of a Torah curriculum.[3]

iv) סוד *(sod)* – the kabbalistic understanding of the text, revealing the mystical secrets of Torah.

These are merely the broadest categories. Our Sages have taught us that there are seventy ways to interpret Torah, and the commentators go further to say that each of those seventy ways has many sub-approaches.[4]

The more we appreciate the variety of approaches, and the greater the array of tools we have at our disposal, the more exciting our learning experience will become. The Malbim, for example, in his brilliant work *Ayeles Hashachar*, lists no fewer than 613 tools for interpreting Torah text!

In this connection, it is important to realize that different commentaries stress different approaches to interpretation. There is a vast difference between studying the commentary of, say,

---

2. The word פרדס literally means orchard. When we enter the פרדס, delicious fruits are waiting to be picked and eaten.
3. For an elucidation of the principles, see the end of tractate *Berachos* [Vilna Edition].
4. See *Zohar*, Bereishis 47b; *Sefer Hachinuch* 95.

R. Samson Raphael Hirsch, with his emphasis on *pshat,* and the *Sfas Emes,* who concentrates on *remez.*

Different commentaries will resonate with different students and it is important to offer students a variety of approaches so that they can discover which they find the most rewarding. Perhaps a different commentary can be learned each year to keep Chumash study fresh and stimulating.

Learn the original Hebrew text

It is impossible to appreciate the subtlety and beauty of Chumash without learning it in the original Hebrew. Many of the nuances, connections and references are lost in translation. There is no substitute for learning Chumash in the language in which the Torah was given to us!

A working knowledge of Hebrew grammar is essential. Many of the tools which are discussed in this book assume this knowledge. Students need to be able to identify the root of every word as well as the tenses, *binyanim,* prefixes and suffixes.

There is no question that this requires effort on the part of the teacher and the student, but it is, without a doubt, worth it.

It requires work, but it is worthwhile

Learning from the original Hebrew text can be a great challenge. As teachers, we should convey that learning Torah is not simple and requires effort. However, the investment is worthwhile because we will discover remarkable insights!

There is a plethora of books that offer bite-sized *vorts* on the *parshah.* These are no subsitute for the thrill and the challenge of real Chumash study. As our Rabbis have taught us:

> *According to the effort is the reward.*[5]

---

5. *Avos* 5:22.

The efforts made in studying Chumash will be amply rewarded by the gains. Besides the benefits for Torah study itself, it provides a vital lesson for all areas of life.

Questions, questions, and more questions

A crucial element in creating excitement is questions. The students must be encouraged to approach the text with no preconceived notions and to ask all the questions that they can. If one has a question, one will be interested in hearing the answer!

Several of the most famous of commentaries start sections of commentary with a series of questions that arise from reading the text. These include the commentaries of Abarbanel, Alshich and Malbim.

The students should ask *every* question they have on the text before any commentary is opened. When they see that they have anticipated many of the questions of the commentators, they will feel empowered, and be genuinely interested to discover the answers.

Show the relevance

There are many practical lessons which can be gleaned from the study of Chumash. When these lessons are highlighted, the students realize that the study of Chumash is relevant to their lives.

For example, the story of Eliezer searching for a wife for Yitzchak provides many insights into what one should look for in a potential spouse.

There is scarcely a section of Chumash that does not contain an abundance of lessons as to how to live a life based on *mussar* and self-perfection.

Maintain surprise

There should be an element of surprise in our learning – the "WOW" factor. If we have asked questions and are putting in effort and learning in the correct manner, using the tools of Chumash interpretation, we will be astonished and thrilled time after time by the discoveries we make.

We should not "give the game away," but facilitate the students' arrival at solutions, as much as possible, by themselves.

Be passionate and the students will follow

Teachers themselves have to be excited by the subject matter they are teaching and, in addition, must realize the huge responsibility that rests on them to transmit the beauty and excitement of Torah, spark their students' excitement and whet their appetite for further study.

Therefore, those sections of Torah and those commentaries which animate the teacher are the ones which should be taught. This should, of course, be balanced by the teacher's understanding of what is likely to interest the students.

It is appropriate to quote the Midrash:

> *Resh Lakish taught, "One who speaks words of Torah and they are not as pleasing to the listeners as a bride is to her groom at the time of their wedding, it would have been better not to have said them."*[6]

This gives an idea of how exciting the study of Torah is expected to be!

Teachers of Torah *do* have an enormous responsibility. However, as those who transmit the word of G-d, we also have a huge privilege. I have no doubt that we will receive a generous dose of divine assistance in the task!

---

6. *Midrash Rabbah, Shir Hashirim* 4:23.

Dedicated in loving memory
of our parents and grandparents,

Isidore and Belle Glastein
Isaac and Frieda Sutton.

With love,
Dr. Cary and Deborah Glastein,
Ian and Sophie Glastein

This book would not have become a reality
without the encouragement and support of friends.
I would like to thank those who helped it happen:

Mr. Jacob Bleakley
Mr. & Mrs. Richard Bodziner
Mr. & Mrs. David Bratslavsky
Rabbi & Mrs. Jack Cohen
Mr. & Mrs. Alexander Fleischer
Mr. & Mrs. Amit Friedlander
Mr. Jacob Kafka
Mr. & Mrs. Pesach Klibenow
Mr. Yonatan Kor
Mr. Zac Miller
Mr. & Mrs. Judd Millman
Mr. Yona Schutz
Mr. & Mrs. Noah Siegel
Mr. & Mrs. Shlomo Simkins
Mr. Kenneth Soloway
Mr. & Mrs. Josh Steineger
Mr. Jared Weiss
Mr. Michael Yaschik
Mr. & Mrs. Shaul Yechezkel